How to coach
BADMINTON

How to coach
BADMINTON

Jake Downey

WILLOW BOOKS
Collins
8 Grafton Street, London W1
1990

Willow Books
William Collins Sons & Co Ltd
London • Glasgow • Sydney • Auckland
Toronto • Johannesburg

First published 1990

Text copyright © Jake Downey 1990
Copyright © William Collins Sons & Co Ltd 1990

A CIP catalogue record for this book is available from the British Library.
ISBN 0 00 218320 X
paperback
ISBN 0 00 218370 6
hardback

Commissioning Editor: Michael Doggart
Senior Editor: Lynne Gregory
Designer: Peter Laws
Illustration: Craig Austin

This book was designed and produced by
Amanuensis Books Ltd
12 Station Road
Didcot
Oxfordshire
OX11 7LL

Originated, printed and bound in Hong Kong by Wing King Tong Co. Ltd

The pronoun 'he' has been used throughout and should be
interpreted as applying equally to men and women as appropriate.
It is important in sport, as elsewhere, that women and men should
have equal status and opportunities.

CONTENTS

THE AUTHOR

Jake Downey is a former top class player and now a B.A. of E. Senior coach who has coached the England Uber Cup teams of 1972 and 1975 as well as many of England's world class players, including several All England singles and doubles champions. He has written and presented the popular BBC TV series *Better Badminton*. He is now Director of Coaching of the B.A.of E. and has written this introductory guide for coaches interested in learning more about coaching the modern game.

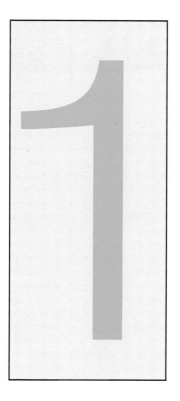

GETTING STARTED AS A COACH

Getting Started as a Coach

If you have taken this book from a shelf to browse through or have bought it to read and learn from then you already have an interest in people and the game - the first requirements of a good coach. Now read on and let me see if I can interest you still further and help you to become one of the many people who gain pleasure from coaching others in badminton.

No doubt you have some previous experience of the game, either as a player or as a spectator, and probably already think it is an enjoyable game to play or to watch. If you haven't played the game and would still like to be able to teach it, this book will help you to do so. In fact, in learning to teach the game it is more than likely that you will also learn to play it. First let's have a general look at what you need to know about the game and the people who play it.

There are several questions non-players usually ask about badminton. What is it ? Why play it ? What do you need to play it ? And how do you play it ? Players, on the other hand, usually want to know how they can become better players.

If you are going to become a coach you must be able to provide the answers. Let us take each question in turn and find out what each one entails.

What is Badminton ?

It is a hitting game which evolved from the ancient game of battledore and shuttlecock. Games similar to battledore and shuttlecock had been played for recreation in one form or another for hundreds of years, the idea being to cooperate to see how many times the players could hit the shuttlecock to and fro without it hitting the ground. The idea changed from one of cooperation to one of competition when the players began to hit the shuttle to the ground on their opponent's side of the court.

The name badminton comes from Badminton House, the Gloucestershire (now Avon) estate of the Duke of Beaufort where, in 1873, it is claimed some army officers on leave from India amused themselves by playing the game. The first set of rules was formed in 1873 in Poona and added to over the next few years.

The game continued to develop in different forms in various countries until in 1893 the Badminton Association of England (BA of E) was formed, and a uniform set of the Laws of Badminton was published. In 1934 the International Badminton Federation (IBF) was formed, the association of the countries which play badminton.

The most prestigious tournament, the All England Championships, was first held in 1899. It takes place annually and is attended by the top players from all over the world. Until 1977 when the IBF organized the first formal world championships in Malmo the All England Championships were considered to be the unofficial World Championships. The IBF world championships are now held every two years. Other major championships are the Commonwealth Games, the European Championships, the Asian Championships and many grand prix tournaments. There are also major team championships - the Thomas Cup for men and the Uber Cup for women - which are held every two years. In 1992 badminton gains full recognition as an Olympic sport.

Why Play Badminton ?

The only real answer to this question is to be found by playing the game and discovering for oneself. If, however, the questioner requires persuasion then one possible answer is that the game is both enjoyable and interesting to play. There are a number of reasons for this.

• It is an *easy* game to learn as the design of the shuttlecock causes it to slow down in the air and enables the players to rally successfully. As a result it is possible to play the game from the start and gain immediate *satisfaction* from doing so.

• It is a *social* game as it can be played by people of all ages.

• It is a *recreational* game providing a large range of physical movement which exercises the body and gives the players the feeling of fitness and wellbeing so essential for good health. There is the opportunity to perform sprints, twists and turns, bends and stretches, jumps and landings, and quick changes of direction as well as using a large range of strokes to hit the shuttlecock with more or less power. The variety of movement appeals to many players.

• It is a *challenging* game as it tests the players' physical skill, intelligence and imagination, character and fitness in an attempt to beat the opponents. Herein lies more interest and enjoyment for enthusiastic games players for the task of trying to outwit the opposition can raise challenges which must be overcome in the game.

• It is an excellent *spectator* sport which nowadays receives good TV coverage and provides the opportunity for more people to see the top players in action. The more people know about the game, the more they will understand and appreciate its fascination and the more they will come to enjoy it.

• It is an *enjoyable* game within sport. Even though the point of any competitive game is to try and win, the reason the majority of us participate in sport is for our enjoyment - for fun, something which badminton offers lots of scope for. Players may play the game seriously and try their best to win, otherwise it would hardly be worth playing, but the result is not the most important issue. What matters most is that players have a good challenging game and come off court feeling better for playing it.

• It is a very *popular* game which is well organized and administered to give players every opportunity to play and enjoy the game at whatever level they aspire to.

What is Needed to Play Badminton ?

You require the basic equipment of rackets, shuttles, appropriate clothing and footwear as well as courts to play on, other players, some skill in hitting the shuttle and moving on the court, some knowledge of the rules (the Laws of Badminton) and how to play the game.

Let's start with the equipment as this can make the difference to players' safety and enjoyment of the game and their success in it.

1. The Racket

Most racket frames these days are made completely of lightweight materials like carbon graphite or a very lightweight metal (used only in the head). A racket should be reliable and easy to control and for this reason there are a number of factors to consider:

• **The weight**: rackets weigh between 95 and 115 grams. As a light racket is easier to control than a heavy racket, you should recommend a racket which is about medium weight.

• **The balance**: a racket can be light or heavy in the head or evenly balanced. It is easier to control a racket that is evenly balanced or lighter in the head. Test the balance of a racket by resting it on your finger at a point midway between the head and the handle.

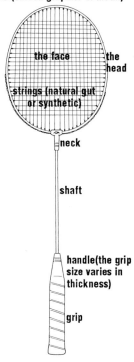

frame (carbon graphite or metal)

the face

the head

strings (natural gut or synthetic)

neck

shaft

handle(the grip size varies in thickness)

grip

The racket
Left: Testing the balance

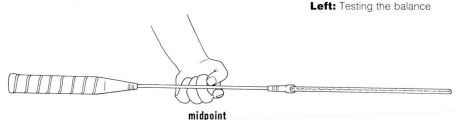

midpoint

11

The head goes down if heavy and up if light. Recommend a racket which is evenly balanced or head light.

• **The handle**: the thickness of the handle (measured around its circumference) usually ranges between three and five inches though it can be any size. This is also known as its *grip size*. A large handle requires the player to grip mainly with the palm of the hand whereas a small handle enables the player to grip mainly with the fingers. As finger control is so important in the game, you should recommend a grip size which allows the player to spread the hand comfortably around the handle and grip it mainly with the fingers.

• **The grip**: this is made of leather, synthetic or towelling material which is wrapped around the handle. It is easy to remove the grip and replace it with a different type. The type of grip used should make it easy and comfortable to hold the racket and control the racket head. Recommend a grip which feels comfortable and secure in the hand. If the players want to use a towelling grip because they sweat a lot in play, advise them to remove their existing grip first so as not to increase the grip size.

• **The strings**: strings are made from natural gut or synthetic fibres and vary in thickness and tension. The more tension that can be applied to the strings, the more the force that can be applied to the shuttle. The thinner the strings, the more a player can feel the contact with the shuttle. The thinner the strings and the greater the tension, the more likely are the strings to break and they can be expensive to replace. Recommend strings which are of medium thickness and medium tension as these should last longest.

• **The price**: you should recommend that players buy a well-known brand of racket in the medium price range as then they should be able to find rackets which satisfy all their requirements. Tell the players to try out several rackets in the sports shop by miming the hitting of the shuttle, swishing the racket about to experience the feel of different rackets until they find one that feels right for them.

2. Shuttlecocks

There are two types, feathered and plastic. Feathered shuttles are more enjoyable to play with but cost more and break more easily. They are made of varying speeds ranging from slow (73 grains weight) to fast (85 grains weight). Plastic shuttles are cheaper and are usually made in three different speeds: fast, medium and slow. There are a number of speeds because the shuttle is affected by the air temperature. In a cold hall the air is more dense, so you need a fast shuttle. In a warm hall the air is less dense, so you need a slower shuttle. Read Law 4 (page 117-8) on how to test a shuttle.

3. Clothing

Badminton involves a wide range of physical movement and can be a very active game so the clothing worn should be comfortable and allow freedom of movement. There is plenty of sports clothing around these days and inexpensive items such as football shorts and T-shirts are adequate for play. A jogging suit is ideal for warming-up quickly before or in play, as well as keeping warm between games.

4. Footwear

Badminton requires quick footwork when starting and stopping, changing direction, and jumping and landing. As the players improve they will find that their feet and knees can take quite a pounding unless they wear shoes which provide adequate friction on the floor surface and cushion the shock of hitting the ground. Recommend that players wear socks which fit comfortably and buy shoes which are well-cushioned and allow them to get a good grip on the floor.

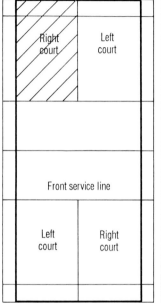

Singles court with service areas

Doubles court with service areas

How to Play the Game

You should be familiar with the Laws of Badminton which give you information about how to score and play the game if you are to teach others to play it. The Laws (the rules of the Game) are included (see page 114) for constant reference as it is unlikely that you will remember them all. First, though, let us obtain a basic idea of the game and how it is played.

• **A description of the game**: the game is played by opposing players on a rectangular court divided into two halves by a net. Two players make a singles game and four players make a doubles game (men's, ladies' and mixed).

The players try to win a rally by using their rackets to hit the shuttle over the net and down to the floor on their opponents' court. A contest is the best of three games which are played up to 15 points except in ladies' singles which are played up to 11 points. At the end of each game the players change ends. See the Laws (pages 113-128) for more detailed information.

• **Beginning a game**: to begin a contest the players toss for the choice of service or ends. The player who wins the toss has the choice of (i) serving first; (ii) not serving first; (iii) ends.

The player who serves the shuttle first is known as the server or *serving side*; the player who receives the serve is known as the receiver or *receiving side*.

• **Scoring in the game**: only the serving side can add points to their score and so each side tries to win the service. Once in possession of the service, players can add a point to their score each time they win a rally. Both singles and doubles players do this by hitting the shuttle to the ground on the opponents' side of the court or if the opponents are unable to return the shuttle into play. If the receiving side wins a rally, the score remains the same but the receiving side gains the service and with it the chance to

Order of service - the singles game

add points to their score. In doubles play the receiving side would have to win two rallies before they gained possession of the service.

• **Order of service - the singles game**
The game is played by two players, A and B. The game begins with the score at love-all (0-0).

1. Player A has won the toss and serves first from his right service court, diagonally opposite to Player B.

2. Player A wins the first rally and adds a point to his score - the score becomes 1-0 to Player A.

3. Player A moves to the left service court and serves diagonally opposite to Player B. (The receiver must stand diagonally opposite the server.)

4. Player A wins the rally and the score becomes 2-0. Player A moves again to serve from his right service court diagonally opposite to Player B.

5. Player B wins the next rally and so wins the service. The score remains the same.

6. Player B now serves from his right service court diagonally opposite to Player A.

7. Player B wins the rally and the score becomes 1-2 (the server's score is always stated first).

It follows that the players stand in the service court related to the score. The players stand in their right hand court if the server's score is an even number and in their left hand court if the server's score is an odd number.

• **Order of service - the doubles game**
This is slightly more complicated but the same rule applies about changing the service court as a point is won. At the start of the game only one player of the serving side is allowed to serve and continues to do so until he loses the serve to the other side. From then on both players on each side have a turn to serve when their side is in possession of the service. The side gaining possession of the service always start their turn at serving from the right court. Here follows a game between pair A and B and pair C and D:

1. Player A serves diagonally opposite to Player C. The serving side wins the rally and the score becomes 1-0.
2. Player A moves to the left court and serves diagonally opposite to Player D and continues to serve diagonally opposite to each opponent in turn until that serve is lost.
3. If Player A was serving to Player D from the left court before he lost the service, he must remain in that court to receive service as long as the opponents possess the serve.
4. Whatever the state of the serve, only the serving side may change from one court to the other in order to serve to each player of the opposing side. The receiving side must remain in the court that they occupied prior to losing the service.

   This is a simple account which explains the formal procedure in the game; a more detailed account is given in the Laws. When you are teaching players to play the game, it is not always

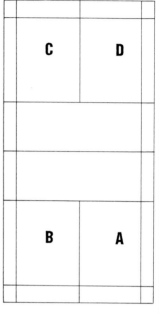

Order of service - the doubles game

GETTING STARTED AS A COACH

necessary to follow the formal procedure and you may (as shown in the lessons in this book) organize games that do not do so.

Where to Play

Most, if not all, sport and leisure centres provide badminton courts which can be booked by the public. Most local authorities organize regular evening classes for people to learn the game and play regularly.

The Badminton Association of England (BA of E) organizes courses for beginners and players of all ages and levels of play. In addition there are many clubs in each town and county affiliated to the BA of E who want more players to join as members.

Recommend to your players that they visit the local sports centre, or write to their Borough Council Educational or Recreational Department or the BA of E for information.
The address is:

The Coaching Department
Badminton Association of England
National Badminton Centre
Bradwell Road
Loughton Lodge
Milton Keynes MK8 9LA

YOUR WORK AS A COACH

Your Work as a Coach

If you are going to take on the job of a coach then you should be aware of what this entails. In this book we are primarily concerned with teaching people how to play badminton, which implies that:

1. You know about the game and how to teach it.
2. You understand how people learn.
3. You know how to plan and arrange what you will teach the players.
4. You know how to communicate with the players.
5. You know how to organize the players in each lesson.
6. You know how to ensure that players attain their satisfaction from playing: for example, enjoyment, interest, challenges and achievements.
7. You must ensure that the environment is safe for play, i.e. the floor surfaces, the surroundings, the lighting, the net and the organization of the other players, as all these features may be potential sources of risk to players' safety.

There is a great responsibility in taking on the job of coach and it is not an easy task to teach others how to play badminton. But just as thoughtful and keen players learn by having a go and improve with practice and experience, so do coaches.

There are similar reasons for coaching as there are for playing, social, enjoyable, interesting and challenging.

The challenge is a constant one for any coach. Coaching is a continuous process of **problem solving** - the problems of making learning easy for the learner; of communicating in such a way that the learner cannot fail to understand what is being said; of saying the right thing at the right time; of teaching the parts of the game in the right order for a particular learner; of stimulating and maintaining interest and providing enjoyment and satisfaction. It is success in these aspects of coaching that provides coaches with their satisfaction and enjoyment. It is a fascinating craft.

I am telling you these things not to put you off coaching but to prepare you for what is to come. If you enjoy helping others, then you will enjoy coaching badminton. You may find that coaching tests your character as well as helping to develop it. You may expect to be frustrated at your failure to get things over first time or at all. You may be irritated or confused by the player who doesn't seem to comprehend what you want, or appears to have got it right and then cannot do it immediately you move on to something else. Coaches require patience, tolerance, empathy, imagination and humour. They need to be questioning, analytical, creative, adventurous, persevering, caring and encouraging.

Players take time to learn how to do things and to understand how to play the game skilfully. There is no guarantee that they will learn something the first time a coach teaches it to them. Coaches must expect to experience all sorts of difficulties in their work and for this reason they should be continually studying on and off court to master their craft. But like all teaching, when the player actually learns something and knows it - then Eureka! - there is a tremendous feeling of satisfaction that you, the coach, have achieved something and all the struggle is forgotten - until the next one.

YOUR WORK AS A COACH

To make life a little easier for you, I have designed this book in a way that will lead the coach gradually into coaching. There should be sufficient information for you to help players play the game and become quite competent in doing so.

If there is one piece of advice I would ask you to bear in mind at all times, it is: **take your time!** There is no hurry - you are not in a race. You should travel at the pace the player is capable of going or is prepared to go at on some occasions. Enjoy your experiences!

TEACHING THE GAME

Teaching the Game

There are several major stages most players will experience in learning to play badminton as to some extent all learners travel a similar road. Once players have passed through these stages they may return to any one of them as necessary to work on particular aspects of their game.

Stage One
They will learn to hit the shuttle and rally. This presupposes that players will learn the following:
1. To judge the speed and the trajectory of the shuttle in flight, judge the distance of the racket from the shuttle and coordinate body movements to use the racket to hit the shuttle to a desired place on the other side of the net.
Note: Some learners find this difficult at first and need simple practices to perform in addition to useful and encouraging advice.
2. To rally with a practice partner.
3. To play a simple game.

Stage Two
They will learn a range of basic stroke-moves as they learn to manoeuvre their practice partners around the court and away from a central court position. There are three different approaches to coaching this stage:
1. The emphasis could be placed on their practice partner or opponent, the OTHER PLAYER, and the **outcome** of their actions as they try to manoeuvre the other player out of position:
• as far away from the net as possible
• as near to the net as possible
• to the right and the left of the court
2. The emphasis could be placed on THEMSELVES, i.e. their own actions in hitting the shuttle and in directing it to different places on the court, without much conscious thought being given to the other player.

This would entail:
• Hitting the shuttle from the space around them:
- Above and below
- In front of the body
- To the right and left side of the body
• Directing the shuttle
- Upwards or downwards
- To the right and left sides of the court
• Hitting the shuttle to land at the back of the court or near to the net.
• Making the shuttle travel quickly or slowly through the air.
• Positioning themselves on the court so as to control the court space and to travel easily to hit the shuttle from any part of it.
3. A combination of the first and second approaches could be used as you could teach learners by combining the two or alternating between them as you decide.

Stage Three
They will learn how to play their opponents in a game. This entails learning:
1. The basic tactical moves and when to use them.
2. How to use them to outwit the opponent.
3. What positions to take up to cover the opponent's moves.
4. How to play singles and doubles (level and mixed).

Stage Four
They will learn how to improve their skill in performing the moves, in moving on the court and in playing their opponents. This entails learning:
1. The basic hitting techniques and a larger range of the stroke-moves.
2. Footwork and the body skill components.
3. How to practise.

Comments
These are the logical stages in learning when the emphasis is placed on teaching people to play the game as soon as possible. In a game the focus is always on what one player does to out-manoeuvre the other player(s) in order to win. In this way the importance of skill in using the racket and in moving on the court becomes more apparent to learners. Practice, therefore, becomes more meaningful because it relates directly to the player's needs to play the game well.

In this way interest is aroused and enjoyment is increased. **The focus of this book is on how to play the opponent(s) in singles and doubles. All your coaching should be directed towards this end.**

Early lessons

The lessons that follow are designed to enable you to introduce and develop the various aspects of badminton to beginners in logical stages. Each lesson may be repeated several times before progressing on to the next lesson. The rate of progress should be determined by the competence and the interest of the players. The lessons will be suitable for a coach working with one player, or with a group of players organized to play in pairs.

In experiencing these lessons, players will acquire skill in hitting the shuttle and moving about the court as they also develop their skill in outwitting their opponent(s). They will learn most of the strokes, positional play and how to use the strokes to make tactical moves in a game.

Before commencing a lesson it is the responsibility of the coach to ensure that the playing conditions are safe for the players.

Safety

At the start of each lesson you should check the playing environment for safety so as to reduce the possibility of any injuries occurring. As a coach you have a moral responsibility to look after the players in your care and you may also be legally liable for accidents which occur unless you have taken due precautions.
• **Floor surface:** Check for splinters or cracked boards if a wooden floor and for loose dust on any floor surface.
• **Surrounds:** There should be a space of about four feet between the back line and any surrounds and at least three feet between the side lines and any surrounds. If this is not the case, warn the players to take care when near any surrounds which are close to the court and special care if the surrounds comprise any obstacles such as windows, chairs or benches. Make sure that the players have not discarded any clothing too close to the court. Advise players not to try to hit the shuttle if they consider that they might risk colliding with an obstacle or another player.

• **The net:** Check that there are no spaces between the netting and the posts and that there are no large holes in the netting for the shuttle to pass through. If the shuttle can pass through the net it poses a potential risk for eye injuries to occur. If there are l. : holes, then change the net or warn players about them and remind them to be careful.
• **Lighting:** Ensure that there is sufficient lighting to see clearly.
• **Footwear:** Be alert for players with footwear inadequate for the floor surface and advise them accordingly.

FIRST LESSONS

First Lessons

Comments and Advice

Let me remind you that these lessons are for complete beginners at Stage One who will vary in their skill in hitting the shuttle. Most beginners are quite happy just to get on the court and try to hit the shuttle back over the net, then to rally and finally play a game of sorts. They will learn by **having a go** and trying to see what they can do. At this stage they do not want much formal instruction about how to hold the racket and hit the shuttle. They will be interested in exploring possibilities and trying out ideas, and will welcome suggestions about how and where to hit the shuttle as long as it does not take time away from hitting the shuttle.

You should not, therefore, clutter up or confuse the players with too many instructions or demonstrations at this stage. Simply give them a task, an idea, to work on and let them get on with it while you remain discreetly in the background observing them and offering the occasional helpful suggestion when appropriate.

You may have to step in and help a player who is experiencing frustration and becoming irritated at being unable to hit the shuttle. Advice, instruction and/or practical help may be necessary to overcome this initial difficulty. Later (page 35) I shall suggest some ways of helping such a player.

Each lesson entails a **plan** which includes its **aims**, the **lesson content** you believe will achieve those aims, and how you will **organize** the players on the court. The aims comprise a list of the things you want the player(s) to learn or experience in the lesson. These will include several tasks and practices for the player to do. The practices will be either:

(a) **cooperative practices** in which the players help each other to learn, or

(b) **competitive practices** in which the players test themselves against each other.

At the end of each lesson you should reflect on and evaluate what you did, and whether or not you achieved your aims. After evaluating your lesson you can then plan the next lesson.

Before starting the lessons let us consider the organization of the players on the court as this may present you with some problems. The first priority is **safety** followed by teaching the **content** and achieving your **aims.** The difficulties arise when you have a class of more than four players to a court. In these lessons it is assumed that the players are allowed on court the whole time to practise with their partners, except when they play games and they have to take turns on the court. Below are some suggestions on how to organize groups of players on the court. If you consider that there are too many for a particular practice at any one time, then you may have to allow them to take turns to practise. Use your common sense to decide this.

Organizing players on the court

Figure 4.1: 4 players   **Figure 4.2:** 6 players   **Figure 4.3:** 12 players

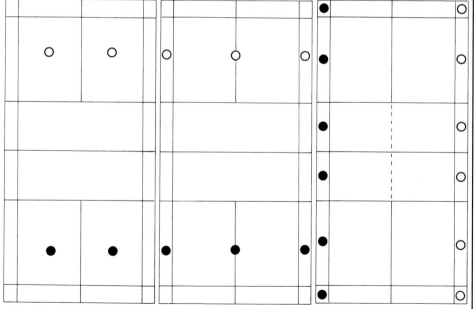

Lesson One

Aims
- To experience badminton
- To learn how to hit the shuttle
- To rally with a partner
- To play a simple game

Organization
The players will practise with a partner, spaced out according to the court space available (see figures 4.1,2,3). Give each pair a shuttle.

Lesson content
Task 1: Practise hitting the shuttle over the net to each other.
Comment: Allow the class to practise in this way and expect a lot of activity as the players hit the shuttle to each other using a variety of actions. They will enjoy this and gain sufficient satisfaction from any success to keep them practising for some time. If you are observing them you will be able to judge when they are ready to start the second task.

Task 2: Try to play a continuous rally and keep the score of your best rally.
Comment: This is a cooperative practice in which the players try to improve and measure their improvement by the score they obtain. It is important that players can see their improvement. Note that they are not in competition with any one but themselves as they try to beat their own best score. As coach you should observe carefully and encourage and praise the efforts and results of each pair.

Task 3: Play a game.
The game is known to coaches as a 'save lives' game. Each player starts with five lives and tries to save those lives by hitting the shuttle back over the net. Failure to do so results in the loss of a 'life'. The game ends when one player has lost all his lives. It is a development from rallying but now gives the players the first experience of a contest.

Before you introduce the game you ought to give the players a few details about how to play the game.

Rules

1. The game will be played in the half-court. See figure 4.4.
2. A player serves until he loses a life and then the opponent serves until he loses a life.
3. The server must hit the shuttle upwards over the net and aim it to cross the front service line and land in the receiver's court. If the shuttle is hit into the net or hit outside the receiver's court, then the server will lose a life.
4. After the serve the shuttle can be hit to anywhere in the opponent's court.

Lesson evaluation

Think about the lesson and whether you achieved your aims:
• Can all the players hit the shuttle?
• Can they all rally?
• Can they all serve the shuttle into the service court?
• Can they all play a game?
• Do all or some players need more practice in hitting the shuttle and rallying before they play games?
• Are some players now ready to play simple games of badminton in which only the server can score points?
• Are some players ready to progress to Stage Two?

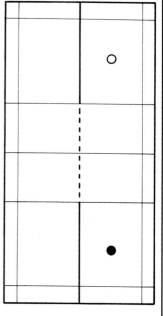

Figure 4.4

Lesson Two

This lesson is similar to Lesson One as players need constant exposure to hitting shuttles and rallying with each other. I would recommend that you repeat Lesson One with several additions.

Aims
• To rally with a partner
• To play a simple game

Lesson content
Task 1: Rally with your partner. Start each rally by hitting the shuttle from below.
Comment: This is a revision of the previous week and allows the players time to try out and practise anything they learned in the previous lesson. You want them to start each rally by hitting the shuttle from below waist height with the racket head held below the level of the hand ready for when they play a game.

Task 2: Rally and try to improve upon your own best score.

Take 3: Play a game of 'five lives'.

Task 4: Play a game of five points.

Lesson evalution
Evaluate the lesson as for Lesson One.

Players with Problems

Occasionally you will meet a learner who finds difficulty in hitting the shuttle. Here are two examples of this:
1. The player who cannot hit it at all, either to start the rally or during the rally.
2. The player who cannot hit it in the centre of the racket and constantly hits the frame.

Problem 1: The player who cannot hit the shuttle.
Possible solution:
1. Place the player in front of you, holding his racket in front of him like a 'frying pan'.
2. Drop a shuttle on the strings of the racket so that the player experiences the feeling of the shuttle striking the racket. Do this several times.
3. Tell the player to lower the racket head slightly and bring it up to meet the shuttle as you drop it. Do this several times until the player can coordinate his movements with the flight of the shuttle. If the player finds this difficult, return to (2) and repeat.
4. Stand a yard from the player and toss the shuttle on to the racket which the player holds as in (1).
5. Tell the player to lower the racket head as in (3) and try to meet the shuttle as you toss it. Repeat this several times until the player can do it.
6. Vary this by tossing the shuttle to the right and the left of the player so he has to make a slight adjustment to the hitting action.
7. Repeat and ask the player to hit the shuttle back to you so that you can catch it.
8. Stand further away to toss the shuttle and ask the player to try to hit it over your head.
Development: Repeat the procedure described in (1), (2) and (3) but this time ask the player to drop the shuttle onto his racket. The shuttle should be held in the finger and thumb of the non-racket hand either by the feathers or by the base. See figure 4.5 and 4.6.

Problem 2: The player who cannot hit the shuttle in the centre of the racket face. Players in this category usually hit the shuttle at the top or bottom of the racket head or the right or left side of the head when they are actually trying to hit the shuttle in the centre of the racket face.

Figure 4.5

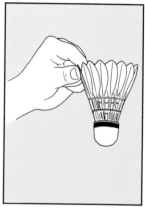

Figure 4.6

Hold the shuttle in the finger and thumb of the non-racket hand (top) or by the base (above).

Possible solution:
If the player hits the shuttle at the top of the racket head then his judgement of spatial distance is out by the length of the distance between the centre of the racket face and the top. See figure 4.7. The solution is:

1. To ask the player to try and hit the shuttle at the bottom of the racket head (Z) which should result in the shuttle being hit in the centre of the racket face (Y).

2. If the shuttle is hit at the bottom of the racket head (Z) then ask the player to try and hit with the top of the racket head (X).

The same principle applies if the player is hitting the shuttle left or right of the centre of the racket face. The correction is to ask the player to try and hit the shuttle on the opposite side of the centre.

Comment: When dealing with such players you must think carefully about the difficulties the player is meeting; try to identify the problem and be patient and encouraging while you are trying to solve it.

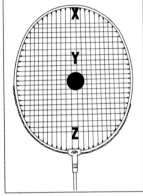

Figure 4.7

LEARNING THE STROKE-MOVES

Learning the Stroke-moves

I wrote in Chapter 3 that there are several approaches to teaching players at Stage Two. You can place the emphasis on what they do to the other player (their practice partner or opponent), or the emphasis can be on themselves, that is, how they hit the shuttle. We will start with the **other player** approach.

The Other Player Approach

Lesson One

¬1s
- To learn how to manoeuvre the opponent out of position
• To rally using a variety of strokes
• To play simple games
Organization:
As for the lessons at the previous stage.

Lesson content
Task 1: **Rally with your partner and practise anything you have learned in the previous lessons.**
Comment: This is a cooperative practice.
It is a sound policy to allow players to start each lesson with a free choice of practice as it gives them the opportunity for revision and reinforcement of things learned previously.

Task 2: **Rally with your partner and try to move your partner as far away from the net as possible.**
Comment: This is a cooperative practice.
You will observe the players hitting the shuttle high and far above their partners' heads as they try to move them away from the net to the RC. Both players might position themselves near to the RC far away from the net to do this. If so, allow them to do so.

Task 3: **Rally with your partner. One player try to move the other as far away from the net as possible while the other tries to bring the partner as close to the net as possible. Decide who does each task first then take turns in trying to do it.**

Comment: This is a cooperative practice.
Start with the players standing in the centre of their midcourts and ask them to try to return to their centres after each hit. It does not matter too much if they do not do this but helps for the next task if they do.

Task 4: Rally with your partner. Try to move your partner as far away from the net or as close to the net as possible.
Comment: Because both players must be ready to travel to the RC or the FC to hit the shuttle, they should return to the MC after hitting the shuttle to get into a position equidistant from the RC and FC. In this way they learn to position themselves in the centre of their court space.

Task 5: Rally with your partner. Try to move your partner as far as you can to the right of the court centre or to the left of the centre.
Comment: Now the players should begin to move their partners away from the centre of the court to the sides. This task is best performed on the full singles court.

Task 6: Rally with your partner. One player try to make your partner hit the shuttle from a high position as far away from the net as possible and one player try to make your partner hit the shuttle from near the ground.
Comment: This is a cooperative practice.
In this rally, suggest that players aim the shuttle towards their partners so that one player hits the shuttle down quickly towards the ground (aim at the partner's knees) while the other player tries to hit it back up into the air.

Task 7: Play a game of five points.
Comment: You should suggest here that if one player can move the other out of position then it will be easier to hit the shuttle down into the remaining space.
In addition, if a player can:
(a) move the other far away from the net as it then becomes

difficult for the other to hit the shuttle down to the ground.
(b) make the other hit the shuttle from below the net in the FC as it forces the other to hit upwards so making it possible to hit the shuttle down to the ground.

General comment: A game is a contest and the point of the contest is to try and win, to defeat the opponent. In performing these simple tasks the players will be experiencing the basic tactical moves in the game with **the emphasis on what to do to the opponent** rather than how to hit the shuttle.

Further Lessons

Lesson One may be repeated several times or just one or two tasks may be selected for practice in each lesson. Evaluate the lessons and decide what the players need. Remember - there is no hurry!

General comments: In these lessons the players have learned to hit up and hit down, to hit the shuttle to the right and to hit it far away from the net. They have experienced some of the strokes and tactics of the game being made conscious of or being told how to hit the shuttle. All their attention has been directed towards what they can do to the other player, which is one of the main features of the game.

The Self Approach

Let us now look at the **self** approach in which players are made aware of how they hit the shuttle. In this approach you will present tasks, give suggestions, and demonstrate and instruct as necessary. The players will experience hitting the shuttle in various ways and learn the names of the basic strokes used as tactical moves in the game. It is a **problem-solving** approach in which the players **explore and discover** ways of hitting for themselves - with a little assistance from the coach at times.

Before we start the lesson I will describe the different strokes so that you recognize which strokes the players will be performing in each task. The word **stroke** refers to both:
(a) the arm and body actions used in hitting the shuttle, and
(b) the trajectory of the shuttle.

With reference to (a), shuttles hit from overhead are called **overhead** strokes and those hit from near the ground are called **underarm** strokes. Shuttles hit from the right side (for a right-handed player) are called **forehand** strokes and those hit from the left side are called **backhand** strokes. See figure 5.1.

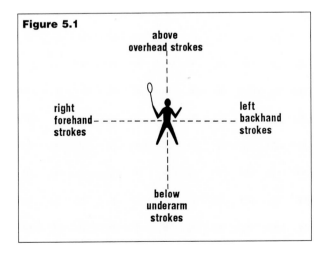

Figure 5.1

above
overhead strokes

right
forehand
strokes

left
backhand
strokes

below
underarm
strokes

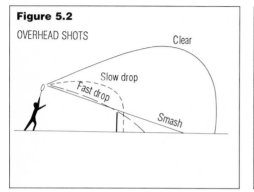

Figure 5.2

OVERHEAD SHOTS

Clear

Slow drop

Fast drop

Smash

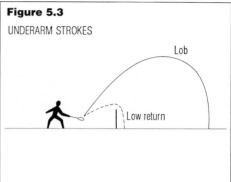

Figure 5.3

UNDERARM STROKES

Lob

Low return

With reference to (b) see figures 5.2, 5.3, 5.4 and 5.5.
Overhead strokes are the **clear** aimed at the RC, the **smash** to the MC and the **fast** and **slow drop** to the FC. See figure 5.2.
Underarm strokes include the **lob** to the RC, and the **low return** to the MC and FC. See figure 5.3.

MC strokes played from net height with a side arm smash action to hit the shuttle at speed horizontally across the net to the MC or RC are called **drives**. See figure 5.4. FC strokes played with the racket head above the hand are called **the kill** (a strong downward hit to the MC) and those played into the FC with the racket head are called **net returns** (see figure 5.5). There are others but for now recognize these when you watch the players practising the tasks you set them.

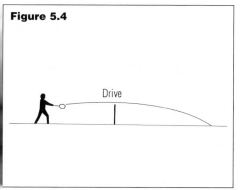

Figure 5.4

Drive

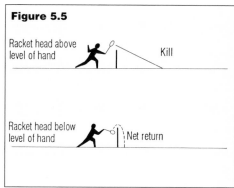

Figure 5.5

Racket head above
level of hand

Kill

Racket head below
level of hand

Net return

General comment: If you reflect for a moment you will realize that it is the clear or the lob that is the stroke used to send the other player out of the central position and as far away from the net as possible; and the dropshot and net replies that bring the other player as close to the net as possible and force him to hit upwards. The smash also forces the other player to hit upwards and, with the drive, also moves him out of position to the sides of the court.

When we talk about what a stroke does to the other player, rather than how the player hits the shuttle, that is, when the stroke is used as a tactical move - we often describe it as a stroke-move. You will see much reference to stroke-moves as we progress.

Lesson One
Aims
• To learn different ways of hitting the shuttle to a partner
• To learn the names of the strokes
• To play a game
General comment: This is a general lesson designed to give the players sufficient expertise in different situations to achieve these aims. For this reason a limited period of time is spent on each task (about five minutes). More time can be spent on each task in subsequent lessons.
Organization
Practice in pairs as for previous lessons.

Lesson content:
Task 1: **Rally with your partner and practise anything you have learned.**
Comment: Allow about five to ten minutes for this.

Task 2: **Find ways of hitting the shuttle high over your partner's head to the RC:**
(a) with an overhead action
(b) with an underarm action
Comment: Allow about five minutes for this depending on the interest shown. The players will rally and perform a crude throwing action using far more strength and movement than is necessary at this stage. They will also have difficulty hitting from their backhand side, particularly from overhead. In fact, most will use a forehand overhead shot to hit the shuttle when it is high.

Task 3: **Find ways of hitting the shuttle just over the net to the FC:**
(a) with an overhead action
(b) with an underarm action as well as hitting it high to the RC
Comment: You will need two objectives here otherwise the players will just stand close to the net and play a net rally. If done properly, they will perform clears, lobs and net shots.

Task 4: **Take turns to find ways of hitting the shuttle down quickly to your partner in the MC:**

Comment: One partner will hit downwards while the other should help by hitting the shuttle up to the RC/MC area. They will find it difficult to hit the shuttle up from the backhand side. At this point they will be ready to learn the basic grips which will be the object of the next lesson.

General comment: The players will have experienced a whole range of strokes and now is as good a time as any to tell them what these strokes are called. Refer to their experience of hitting underarm or overhead to the other player's RC, MC or FC and tell them the names of the different strokes.

Task 5: Play a game of five points.
Comment:. Advise them to use the strokes they have learned and practised to send the other player to RC (as far from the net as possible), to the FC (as close to the net as possible) and to the right and left of the court; and to hit the shuttle down quickly towards the ground.

Lesson Two
Aims:
• To learn the basic grips
• To learn the starting position and the stroke cycle
• To learn the basic stances
• To play a game
Organization:
As for previous lessons.

Lesson content:
Task 1: Rally with your partner and practise the strokes you learned in the previous lesson.
Comment: Players who have been working on their own ways of performing the strokes will still be experimenting and will be quite happy to work on their own ideas. They will have some difficulty in hitting the shuttle from the backhand side and consequently this is a good time to teach them the basic grips.

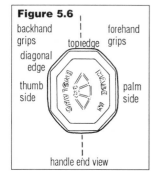

Figure 5.6

backhand grips · forehand grips

top edge

diagonal edge

thumb side

palm side

handle end view

The Basic Grips

The purpose of the different types of grips used to hold the racket handle are to give control of the racket head and face. A racket has two identical faces: the forehand face, when the shuttle is hit as if with the **palm side of the hand**; and the backhand face when the shuttle is hit as if with the **little finger side edge** of the hand or the **thumb.**

You will already have noticed that players have to hit the shuttle from various spaces around the body, ie in front, at the sides above them and near the ground. As the modern racket is very light and requires great finger control, the important rule to remember is never to grip the handle too tightly. Figure 5.6 illustrates the racket handle with the main hand positions.

The basic forehand grip

You can teach the grip as follows:

Method 1: Hold the racket by the neck in the non-racket hand. Place the palm of the racket hand on the strings of the racket. Slide the palm down the racket until the palm is behind the racket handle. Close the fingers and thumb gently round the handle.

Method 2: Hold the racket by the neck in the non-racket hand with the head of the racket pointing forwards and the side edge of the racket frame pointing towards the ground. Shake hands gently with the racket handle.

Note: The fingers can be spread out to allow a more comfortable grip.

Comment: When teaching this grip, bring the players close so that everyone can see your hand position clearly. Demonstrate the grip and how to do it. Let the class have a go while you observe them and make sure that they hold the racket handle correctly. Do the same for the following grips.

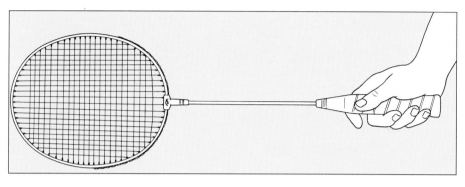

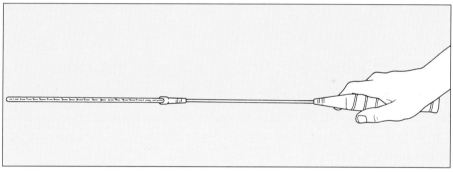

The forehand grip
Top: side view
Above: top view

The backhand grip
Below: side view
Bottom: top view

The basic backhand grip

This is useful for most strokes played from the backhand side.
You can teach this as follows:
Method: Hold the racket handle in the forehand grip. Relax and move your hand over the top edge of the racket handle until the whole thumb is pressed flat against the back edge of the handle. It should now be easy to apply pressure with the thumb on the handle directly behind the backhand face of the racket.

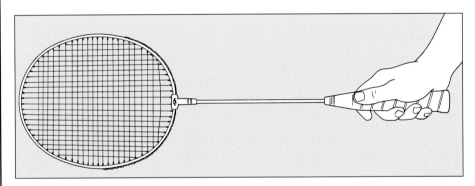

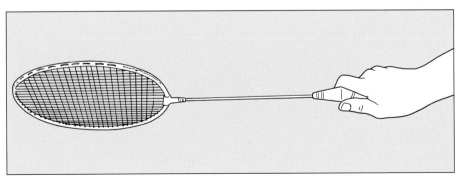

The multi-purpose grip

This is an alternative grip which is simply a slight variation on the basic backhand grip. Many players hold their racket in this grip between strokes and use it for many backhand strokes when they find it difficult to use the basic backhand grip. You can teach this as follows:

Method: Hold the handle in the basic backhand grip. Relax this grip and adjust your hand position until the thumb presses against the diagonal edge of the racket.

The multi-purpose grip
Below: side view
Bottom: top view

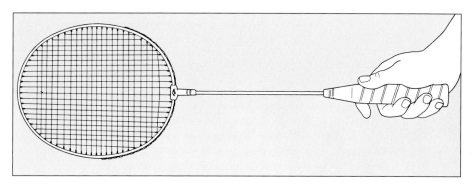

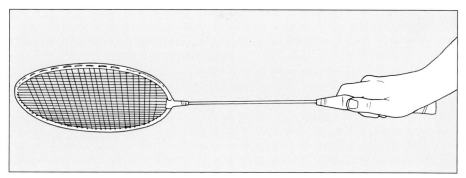

Practices for the Grips

It is important that your players learn the basic grips and can change from one to the other easily. Regular practise on and off court will help them to do this.

Off-court practices

Task 1: **Hold the racket handle in your hand and practise changing from one grip position to another using your thumb and fingers to move the handle around in your hand.**

Comment: This practice is similar to a pianist doing finger exercises on the piano. Players should be able to change from one hand position to another quickly in play.

Task 2: **Spin the racket handle in your hand and practise stopping in one of the basic grips.**

On-court practices

Task 3: **Stand in the midcourt and rally with your partner.**

Comment: Observe the players and help them where necessary. When they have got the general idea in the MC then give them one more task.

Task 4: **Ask your players to rally with their partners and practise using the forehand and backhand grips for overhead strokes and underarm strokes.**

Comment: Allow free practice for this exercise as the players will enjoy exploring their own ways of doing this.

The Starting Position and the Stroke Cycle

It should be apparent to you by now that a good court starting position is in the centre of the MC. From this position players can reach all parts of the court to hit the shuttle. You may also have noticed that some players are late getting to the shuttle because they have not returned to the centre of the MC after their previous hit.

Additionally you might have noticed that some players may be late in preparing their racket to hit the shuttle and that their arm movements seem to lack control. This usually happens when players do not perform a stroke cycle. Let us look at these two aspects in turn and give the players some simple practices which will help them to become more skilful.

Task 5: Rally with your partner. Start in the centre of the MC and return towards there each time you hit the shuttle.
Comment: It will not be necessary to return there on every occasion, for example when playing a net rally in the FC, but on most occasions players will return towards the centre. This is a cooperative practice.

Task 6: Rally with your partner. Start with your racket held in front of you ready to hit the shuttle from anywhere in the space around you; return your racket to your starting position in front of you before you hit the next shuttle.
Comment: If you are to make the players skilful they must perform the full stroke. A stroke comprises of: a racket starting position, a preparation, the hitting action and the recovery back to the starting position, i.e. a complete cycle of movement. It is the performance of this cycle that provides the rhythm and fluency in the performance of a stroke and ensures that the player is prepared each time to hit the shuttle. This simple task ensures that players complete the stroke cycle each time they hit the shuttle. They will certainly notice the difference and the improvement. Once they get the idea, you can always remind them should they forget on occasion. I will say more about this

later when describing some of the essential stroke actions.

Task 7: Rally with your partner. Use your strokes to send your partner to the RC, as far from the net as possible; to the FC, as close to the net as possible; to the sides of the court; to get your partner to hit upwards.
Remember to return to the centre of the MC after hitting the shuttle and to return your racket to its starting position.

Comment: There are several items to remember in this exercise and not all players will remember them. Observe the players practising and remind them as necessary. You should also remind them to change grip for forehand and backhand strokes. Just as important as reminding them to do something is **praising** them when they remember something or do it well.

Basic stances
Defensive stance, front view (right) and side view (far right).
Attacking stance;
forward attacking (below right) and backward attacking (below far right).

The Basic Stances

Once your players have got used to returning to their central starting position in the court you can teach them how they might stand in that starting position. The point to remember is that they will stand positioned ready to cover certain replies from their opponents. There are several basic stances:

The defensive stance
If they had hit a clear to their opponent then they should stand ready to defend against a possible smash which would usually be the strongest move they would have to prepare for. They would adopt a **defensive stance**, like a catcher, ready to move sideways. See opposite.

The attacking stance
(a) Forward attacking stance: If they had hit the shuttle down, or caught the opponent out to some extent and expected a weak reply, they might stand positioned with the racket foot slightly ahead of the other foot ready to spring forwards to attack the reply. See opposite.
(b) Backward attacking stance: If they had hit the shuttle down to the opponent's FC or MC, and expected the opponent to try to

hit the shuttle quickly over their head to the RC, they might stand positioned sideways on with the racket foot behind the non-racket foot ready to travel quickly backwards to hit the shuttle. See illustration on previous page. This is also the stance players adopt when receiving the serve.

Comment: Notice the alertness of each stance in the illustrations: knees slightly bent, weight poised on the balls of the feet, a straight back showing good posture, and head up watching the opponent carefully.

Task 8: Play a game of 5-7 points.
Use your strokes to move your opponent out of position: to the RC (as far away from the net as possible), to the FC as close to the net as possible, and to the sides of the court.

Comment: Once the players start playing a game their focus will be the other players. Consequently they may forget many of the things they have just been practising, i.e. the grips, the stroke cycle, the court starting position and the basic stances. You must expect this and simply note which players have remembered the most and to what extent. Future lessons will require regular practice on all these aspects. Remember - there is no hurry! Simply observe, take note and keep encouraging and helping them to learn and improve.

General comments
These two lessons or parts of them can be repeated until you feel certain that the players are ready to progress to Stage Three. I have found such tasks very useful and often return to these practices even with players who have progressed beyond Stage Two. It is quite common when teaching badminton to progress on and then return to an earlier stage and revise and/or reinforce some aspect of the game.

If the players are now reasonably competent at Stage Two and interested in moving on, you can progress to Stage Three and teach them how to play singles and doubles. We will start with singles because it is easier to teach the basic tactical moves with this game.

COACHING SINGLES

Coaching Singles

So far the players have been largely self-taught as you have structured their playing environment so that they have become steadily more skilful at hitting the shuttle in order to practise with and play against the other player. They have played many games of singles and used their skill and wits to outplay their opponents. Now that they are at Stage 3, we will look more closely at how to use the strokes as tactical moves in singles and doubles. We will discuss singles in this chapter and doubles in the next chapter.

The attraction of singles for many players is that they are on their own in a one to one contest - a test of their skill and intelligence against the other player. Players should learn therefore how to go about trying to win. To do so they must possess some skill in hitting the shuttle and be able to use their strokes as moves to defeat their opponents. The game is quite simple: the purpose being to hit the shuttle to the floor in the opponent's court and to prevent the opponent doing the same in one's own court.

Before we begin teaching players how to use the strokes as moves, you, the coach, should develop a sound knowledge of singles tactics. With this intention let us now examine the game of singles in some detail and consider some methods of teaching players to use tactics.

The Strokes and their Use as Tactical Moves

Tactics and the principles of attack

Whenever a player hits the shuttle over the net he is making a tactical move in the game. As the game is a contest, the point of the move should be to contribute to winning the rally and ultimately the game. To play in this way is to play in accordance with the **principle of attack.** This can be stated as:

> **at all times try to create a situation which will increase your chances of eventually making a scoring hit.**

The strokes are the means by which a player makes the moves in the game. If a player applies the principle of attack in play then the strokes cease to be simple actions and become stroke-moves. Tactics do not exist without the strokes, and the strokes are pointless actions in the context of the game unless they carry out the tactics. Strokes and tactics are inseparable.

The logical structure of the game

The game has a logical structure similar to any other rule-governed game. During a game players will frequently find themselves at different times in different situations. In each situation they have to make a move of sorts in accordance with the rules of the game. In each situation, however, certain moves are **logically possible**, though what is **actually possible** depends on the ability of the players. If players are limited in their ability to make any of the moves possible in a given situation, they will have less choice of moves available to them in that situation. Once the **actual move** is made by the player it may be judged for its **appropriateness** as a good or a poor move in that situation by reference to the principle of attack.

The logical structure of the game is clearly seen in figure 6.1. below.

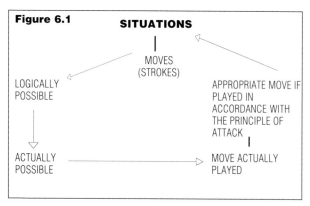

Figure 6.1

SITUATIONS

MOVES (STROKES)

LOGICALLY POSSIBLE

APPROPRIATE MOVE IF PLAYED IN ACCORDANCE WITH THE PRINCIPLE OF ATTACK

ACTUALLY POSSIBLE

MOVE ACTUALLY PLAYED

The situations in the game

As the court is rectangular and divided by a net five feet high it is possible to establish a number of situations in each area of the court. This is done by taking the position of the shuttle in the court relative to the height of the net as the player is about to hit it.

The shuttle is either high or low in the court, that is, above or below the net, or midway, level with the net. The shuttle can be hit down, hit up or hit horizontally.

It becomes easy therefore to identify the RC, MC and FC as the major situations from which the stroke-moves are played. See figure 6.2. It does not take much thought to realize that there are numerous stroke-moves logically possible within each situation. Fortunately these can all be reduced to **three basic moves.**

We have already experienced some of these in the Stage Two lessons.

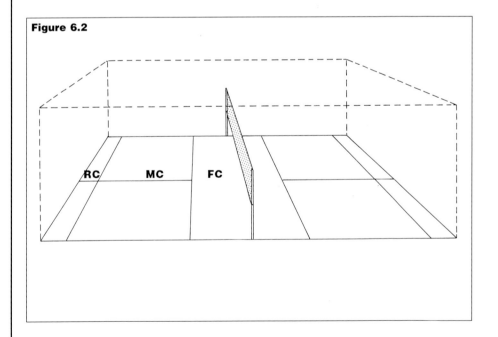

Figure 6.2

THE STROKES AND THEIR USE AS TACTICAL MOVES

The three basic moves against other players
First there are stroke-moves used to send the opponent to the RC.
These are the **overhead clear**, the **underarm lob**, the **drive** and
the **high serve**. There is also the flick serve which we have not yet
experienced. The reasons for playing these moves are:
• To move the opponent out of position away from the centre
• To create space
• To make the opponent less effective

Second there are the stroke-moves used to draw the opponent
into the FC. These are the **overhead dropshot**, the **net replies**
and the **low serve**. The reasons for playing these moves are:
• To move the opponent out of position away from the centre
• To create space
• To force the opponent to hit upwards

Third there are the stroke-moves used to send the opponents to
the sides of the MC. These are the **smash, kill, drive** and **push**.
The reason for playing these moves are:
• To move the opponent out of position way from the centre
• To create space
• To force the opponent to hit upwards
• To make a scoring hit

The stroke-moves played from the situations

Another way of looking at the stroke-moves is to consider those
that are played from the court situation of the player making
them. These are as follows:
Rearcourt (RC): smash, clear and dropshot
Midcourt (MC): smash, drive, push, lob, net reply and the serve
Forecourt (FC): smash, kill, net replies and lob

General comment: If you pause and reflect for a moment you
will realize that you will be familiar with these stroke-moves as
we have already covered them to some extent in the two approaches
taken in Chapter 5, i.e. **the other player** approach and the **self**
approach. At this stage your job is to make the players fully aware
of what they have already experienced. Let us therefore give your

players some games to play which will help to develop their tactical understanding. Before starting them off you should read through each game carefully so that you understand what they have to do. Once you have explained the additional rule in each game, you should ask them the purpose of the move to see if they understand why it is a useful move to make.

Game One
Learning to use the move to the rearcourt
Task: Play a game of half-court singles up to 5-7 points. There is one additional rule: before you can smash, you must have caused the other player to place one foot inside the RC.
Once you have done this, you can use the smash at any time during the rally. If you smash before you do this, you lose the rally.
Note: This rule ensures that one player tries to force the opponent as far away from the net as possible and teaches them also to watch each other's feet to make sure that they have hit the shuttle to the RC.

Game Two
Learning to use the move to the forecourt
Task: Play a game of half-court singles up to 5-7 points. There is one additional rule: before you can smash, you must have caused the other player to place one foot or reach with the racket arm inside the FC. Once you have done this, you can use the smash at any time during the rally. If you smash before you do this, you lose the rally.
Note: This rule ensures that one player tries to move the other out of position into the FC and also forces the other to hit upwards. Once again they learn to watch the opponent and to judge the effectiveness of their stroke-moves.

Game Three
Learning to use the move to the sides of the court
Comment: In this game the players should use all the basic moves to the RC, FC and MC to move the other player sideways out of position. To appreciate the full effect of this move, the players should play singles on the full court.

THE STROKES AND THEIR USE AS TACTICAL MOVES

Task: Play a game of singles up to 5-7 points. There is one additional rule: before you can smash, you must first make the other player travel completely into one side of the court and then immediately into the other side of the court. If you smash before you do so, you lose the rally.

Note: This rule ensures that one player tries to move the other out of position sideways by using the strokes to play straight and cross court moves.

General comments: In all these games, the players learn to make tactical moves with the intention of creating a situation in which they can attempt to make a scoring hit and so win the rally. They learn to apply the principle of attack.

It could be that one player finds it difficult to move the opponent out of position because he cannot perform the stroke very well. In such an instance some help and some practice is required. Read Chapter 9 to find out how the different strokes are performed and how to teach players to move on the court if you think you may have to help the players with instruction and/or advice. You can read that chapter now or later but in the meantime I will describe some useful practices which the players can try out.

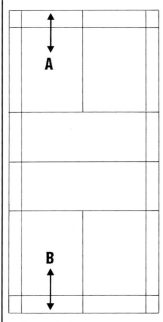

Figure 6.3

Practices for Singles

There are two types of practice included here; technical and tactical. In a technical practice the player focuses on him**self**, ie how he hits the shuttle or moves on the court, whereas in a tactical practice the player focuses on the other player, i.e. what he can do to the other player.

Some practices are a combination of both types. In addition some practices are cooperative in that the players help each other to improve while others are competitive with the players testing themselves out against each other. I will state what type of practice each one is so that you will know where to place the emphasis each time.

First Practice
Aim: To improve the performance of the **clear** as a tactical move
Types of practice: Tactical and cooperative
Instructions: See figure 6.3.
1. The players stand in the positions as shown in the centre of their MCs.
2. Player B serves high to Player A.
3. Player A travels back to RC and hits a forehand clear to Player B, then returns towards the MC.
4. Player B travels back to the RC and hits a forehand clear to Player A and so on.
Duration: The practice ends when each player has been able to make the other player perform a clear with at least one foot in the RC on three to five occasions.
Note: One player may achieve this before the other and it may take numerous hits before both players finally achieve this goal. The players can take rests as necessary and play several rallies to achieve their target.
5. **Variation Practice:** The players practice performing the **backhand clear.**
Note: As the backhand clear is more difficult to perform, for learners, the practice is a purely technical one.
Instructions: The players rally with Player A performing forehand clears and Player B performing backhand clears. The players change over when Player B has hit five backhand clears to the MC or beyond. See figure 6.4.

Second Practice
Aim: To improve the performance of the **lob** and the **dropshot** as tactical moves
Types of practice: Tactical and cooperative
Instructions: See figure 6.5.
1. The players stand in the positions as shown in the centre of their MCs.
2. Player B serves high to Player A.
3. Player A travels to the RC and hits a dropshot into Player B's FC and returns towards the MC.
4. Player B travels forward and performs a lob to Player A's RC and recovers to the centre MC and so on.
Duration: The practice ends when:
• Player B has made Player A perform a dropshot with at least one foot in the RC on five occasions.
• Player A has made Player B perform a lob from the FC on five occasions.
5. Repeat the practice with the players changing their positions.

Figure 6.4   **Figure 6.5**

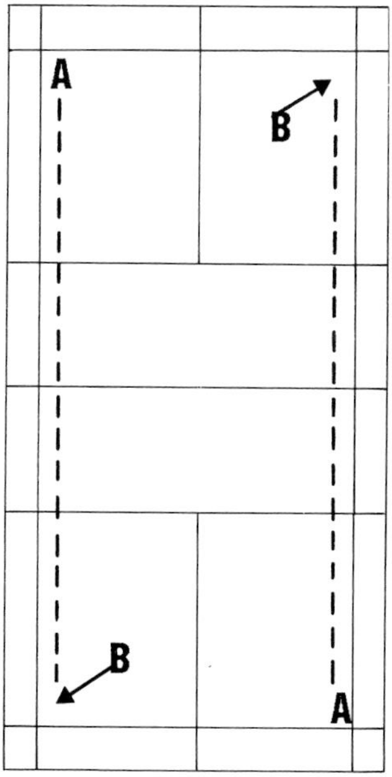

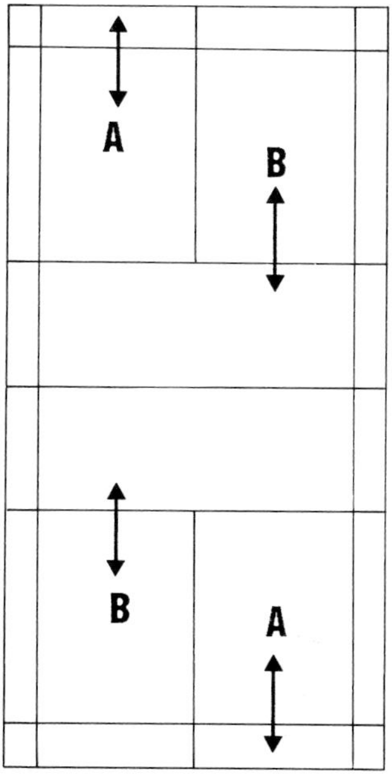

Third Practice
Aim: To improve the performance of the **smash** and the **lob to the smash**
Types of practice: Technical and competitive
Instructions: See figure 6.6.
1. The players stand in the positions as shown in the centre of their MCs.
2. Player B serves high to Player A and gets ready to defend against the smash.
3. Player A travels back to the RC and smashes the shuttle down to Player B's MC.
4. Player B attempts to lob the shuttle to the RC to keep Player A as far away from the net as possible.
Duration: The practice ends when Player A has hit the shuttle to floor in Player B's court on three occasions.
5. Repeat the practice with the players changing their positions.

General comment: You will notice that in each of these three practices the players have been practising performing the three basic moves **from** the RC and basic moves **to** the RC.

Fourth Practice
Aim: To improve the performance of the **FC reply to the smash**
Types of practice: Technical and cooperative
Instructions: See figure 6.7.
1. The players stand in the position as shown.
2. Player B serves high to Player A and gets ready to receive the smash.
3. Player A smashes at Player B and travels forwards to the MC.
4. Player B returns the shuttle to the FC.
5. Player A travels forward and hits the shuttle to Player B and then returns to the MC.
6. Player B lobs the shuttle to the RC and so on.
Duration: The rally continues until Player B has performed five successful returns to the FC with a forehand stroke and five with a backhand stroke. The players then change their positions.

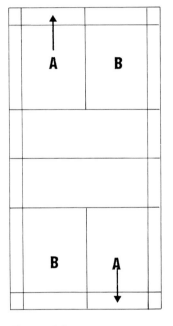

Figure 6.6

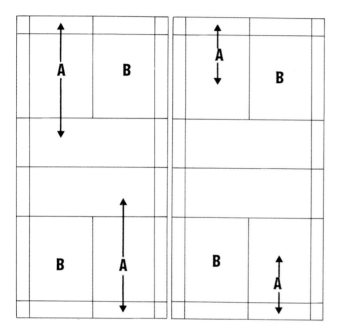

Figure 6.7　　　　　　**Figure 6.8**

Fifth Practice
Aim: To improve the performance of the **MC reply to the smash.**
Types of practice: Technical and cooperative.
Instructions: See figure 6.8.
1. The players position themselves as shown.
2. The practice is similar to the previous one except that Player B aims the shuttle to skim the net and arrive in Player A's MC.
Duration: The rally continues until Player B has perfomed five forehand and five backhand returns to Player A's MC.

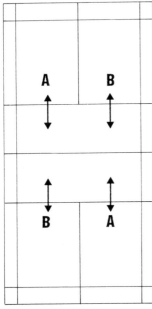

Figure 6.9

Sixth Practice
Aim: To improve the performance of the net replies as tactical moves

Types of practice: Technical and cooperative

Instructions: See figure 6.9.

1. The players stand in the positions as shown behind the short service line.

2. Player A serves the shuttle just over the net into Player B's FC.

3. Player B allows the shuttle to fall below net height and steps forward to hit it just over the net into Player A's FC and travels back behind the short service line.

4. Player A allows the shuttle to fall back below net height and steps forward to hit it back into Player B's FC and then travels back behind the short service line.

Duration: The players continue to rally until they feel that they can return the shuttle accurately over the net into the FC.

5. Five Lives Game
The players rally as before but do so in a five lives games. Each starts with five lives and loses a life each time one fails to return the shuttle over the net into the FC.

Note: Make sure that both players travel back outside the short service line after hitting the shuttle and before the other player does so.

Seventh Practice
Aim: To improve the performance of the **kill in the FC**
Types of practice: Technical and cooperative
Instructions: See figure 6.10.
1. The players stand in the positions as shown - Player A in the FC, Player B in the RC - and rally.
2. Player B hits the shuttle to travel quickly just above net height in the FC.
3. Player A hits the shuttle at Player B.
4. Player B hits the shuttle at Player A, and so on.
5. Player A performs forehand and backhand strokes.
Duration: After ten hits from Player A the players change positions.

Figure 6.10

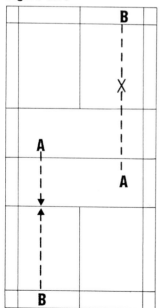

General comments: These are some simple practices which may help the players to perform the basic moves more effectively. By now you should have a good knowledge of the basic moves in the game and why they should be performed well.

It should be quite easy to devise your own technical and tactical practices and make them cooperative or competitive. The important question you should ask of any practice is: will this practice help the player to become better at performing the stroke-moves in a game and contribute to defeating the opponent?

COACHING DOUBLES

Coaching Doubles

Before you begin coaching doubles you should obtain a good working knowledge of how the game is played. Read the following explanation and then I will provide you with some ways of teaching doubles to your players.

There are two forms of doubles - men's and ladies' doubles, known as level doubles, and mixed doubles. We will start with level doubles.

Level Doubles

It is always rather difficult for any coach to teach beginners how to play doubles as they often experience difficulty in learning where and how to position themselves. To beginners, the shuttle seems to be hit to and fro across the net so quickly that they have little time to adjust to the changing situations and often find themselves in the wrong place or late in getting ready to hit the shuttle.

In doubles the emphasis is on attack. It is similar to singles in that the same situations occur in the RC, MC and FC, and similar stroke-moves can be used in accordance with the principle of attack to win each rally. The game differs in that there are two players on each side to make the moves and to cover the opponents' replies. In this respect it is easier to play doubles than singles. The two players must combine to form a team, for if one player makes a move and creates a new situation, it affects both players. The strength of the team depends on cooperation, good positional play and intelligent stroke-moves. Let us begin with a discussion of doubles play and look at how the players work together as a team.

The work of the team

In general the smash is the main stroke-move used to win the rallies. The aim of both sides, therefore, is to create an opportunity to smash. The game is one of continual attack and defence, first by one team and then the other. A doubles team needs to know:
1. How to create an attacking situation and how to attack effectively in that situation.

2. How to defend against any attack and how to regain the attack.

To create an attacking situation one team must force the other team to hit the shuttle upwards. In this situation each team will take up the basic doubles positional formations: **the attacking formation**, the positions one team moves into for attack; and the **defensive formation**, the positions one team moves into for defence.

There are obviously other ways of winning rallies than by the use of the smash, e.g. the drop shot or the clear, which we will discuss later, but in general the smash is the strongest move to use. Let us look at some diagrams which will illustrate the usual doubles positions.

Doubles Positional Play

It is the position of the shuttle in the court, the probable stroke-moves the striker may play and the probable replies of the other team which determine where all the players position themselves.
• The striker's position is determined by the position of the shuttle.
• The opponents' positions are determined by the probable moves the striker may play.
• The striker's partner will take up a position to cover some of the probable replies of the opponents. The striker will move into a position to cover the others.

COACHING DOUBLES

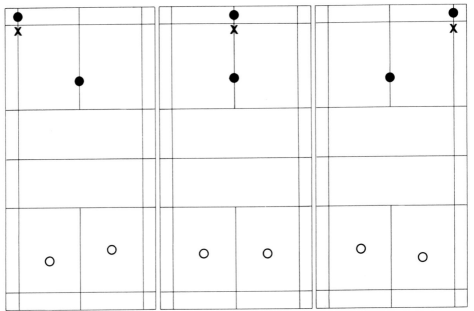

Figure 7.1   **Figure 7.2**   **Figure 7.3**

I have used the following code
throughout this chapter so that you
can grasp the players' positions and
follow their movements more easily:

● signifies the attacking side
O signifies the defensive side
X signifies the shuttle
- - > signifies the movement of the
     shuttle
⟶ signifies the movement of the
     players, i.e. the direction and
     distance they travel

1. RC 'front and back' formation and MC 'sides' formation

Your players should learn the basic RC 'front and back' attacking formation, and the 'sides' defensive formation. Look at the diagrams opposite in figures 7.1,2,3. The three diagrams show the positions of the players in attack and defence when the shuttle is hit from different parts of the RC.

In figure 7.1 the striker is the **back player** in the RC ready to hit the shuttle. The defenders get ready like two goalkeepers or catchers to defend against the smash and position themselves **side by side** in their MC facing towards the striker, and both the same distance from the striker. See illustrations opposite. That is why the defender diagonally opposite to the striker appears to be slightly further forward than his partner.

The striker's partner is the **front player** positioned in the MC ready to intercept and attack the opponent's replies. Now look at figures 7.2 and 7.3 to see how the players adjust their positions slightly when the shuttle is hit from the centre and the left side of the RC.

The players must learn to get into these positions quickly when the shuttle is high in one team's RC area. On page 80 there is a practice that you can use to teach them to do this.

Defensive stances

Finally look at figures 7.4 and 7.5 below which show you what replies to the smash the front player and the back player would try to cover.

Figure 7.4   **Figure 7.5**

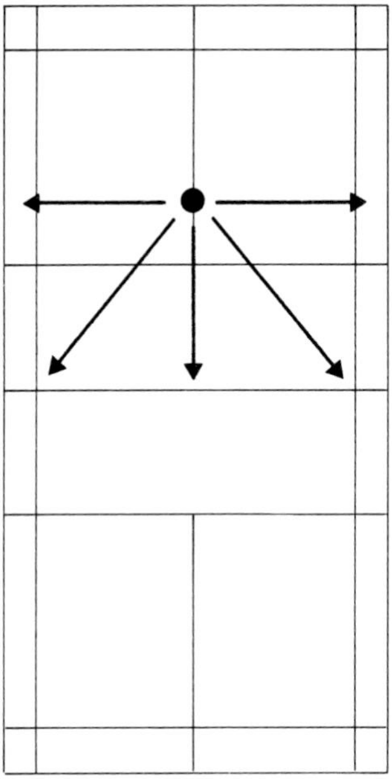

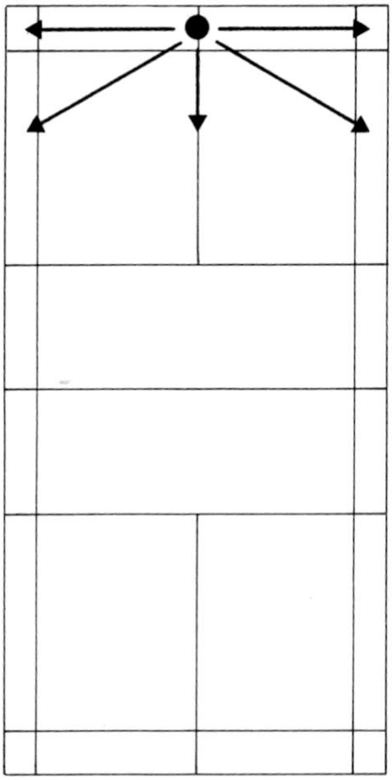

2. The FC 'front and back' attacking formation.

There are two situations in which players take up this formation:
(a) when the shuttle is above the net in the FC
(b) when the shuttle is just below the net in the FC
• Shuttle above the net

Look at figures 7.6,7 and 8.. On each occasion the front player is ready to attack as the striker in the FC and the back player is positioned in the centre of the MC ready to attack any replies which get past the front player. The defenders are in a sides formation ready to defend against the downward hit.

Figure 7.6   **Figure 7.7**   **Figure 7.8**

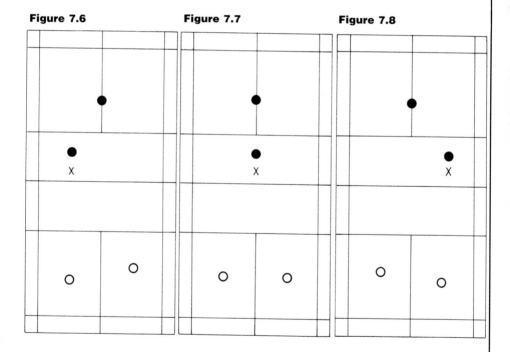

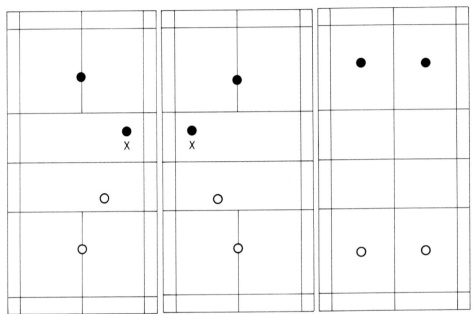

Figure 7.9   **Figure 7.10**   **Figure 7.11**

• Shuttle just below the net height
Look at figures 7.9 and 7.10.. Because the front player (the striker) must hit the shuttle from just below net height, one player from the other team travels forward to become the front player ready to attack the reply. In this situation both teams adopt a FC front and back attacking formation. You will notice a formation similar to this when the teams position themselves for the serve at the start of each rally.

Finally I think we ought to consider a situation which provides a link between the RC attack and the FC attack. On occasions the shuttle is about net height in the MC and both teams take up side positions in the MC ready to attack each other. One team will try to force the other side to hit the shuttle upwards so that they can then take up either a FC or RC front and back attacking formation and force the other team to defend. We call these positions the **sides attacking formation.** See figure 7.11.

Teaching doubles

Playing the first game

Your players can now rally and play some of the basic moves in the game so they will have grasped the general idea of how to play badminton. Doubles appears more complex to play than singles, particularly the scoring and positional play, though the basic moves are identical. I would recommend that you explain how the order of serving works in doubles and then, without more ado, let the players try and play the game. They should enjoy doing so and also obtain some idea of where to or where not to position themselves during the game. In addition, their experience will give you some points of reference when you begin coaching them in doubles play. You should of course read this section on doubles before you begin any lessons with your players.

Task: Play a game of doubles.

Comment: Observe them and compare what they do with what they should be doing to play intelligent doubles. It will help you if you make notes of things they do for you to refer to when you explain to them where they should position themselves to apply the basic tactics. When you have done so you can introduce the following practices and games which are designed to help them to play better doubles.

Shadow Formation Game

The purpose of this game is to teach the players where and how to position themselves for the RC front and back attacking formation and the sides defensive formation.

Position the two teams on court as shown in figure 7.12 (the sides attacking formation). Number the players from one to four. Your task is to call out any number, for example, one, two, three and so on.

The player whose number is called immediately takes up the striker's position in any part of the RC. When the player has done so all the other players immediately adjust their positions accordingly. See figure 7.13.

You should check that they are positioned correctly and if so then call out another number. Each time check the positions and

Figure 7.12   **Figure 7.13**

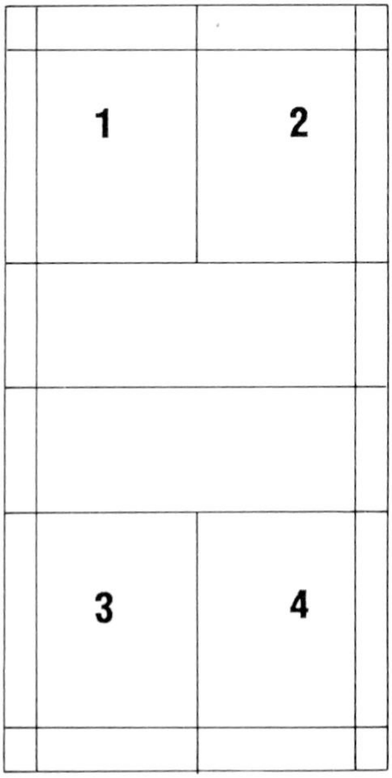

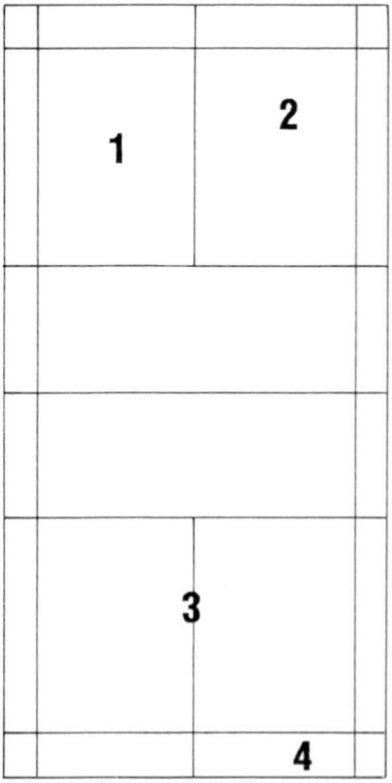

how they are standing, for example, with the front player astride the line in the MC and the defenders standing like catchers. Correct them if they are not in the right positions.

Gradually increase the speed at which you call out the numbers so that they learn to adjust quickly to the changing situations in the game. You may call out the same number several times in which case the striker re-adjusts his position in the RC and the other players adapt accordingly.

No-smash Game

In this game the players play normal doubles with one exception - they are not allowed to smash. If any player smashes the shuttle, the rally ends and is won by the other side.

In this game the players will only use two of the basic moves when the shuttle is high in the MC or RC: they will use the clear and the dropshot. As a result the game is played at a much slower pace, with the players having more time to alter their positions on the court as the situations change within the game. This will become obvious when the players begin to play.

At the start of the game the players should take up the positions for the FC front and back attacking formation. See figure 7.14. This formation is taken up to serve and receive the serve.

The server will serve a low serve or a high serve. When a high serve is played you should see one team take up the RC front and back attacking formation and the other team a sides defensive formation. When a low serve is played, the receiver will either hit the shuttle down softly to the FC or MC if the shuttle is above net height; or play a net reply to the FC, or lob it to the RC, if the shuttle is below net height.

Note: It will take some time for the players to adapt to playing doubles for the first time, and for them to get into the different formations. Be patient and helpful, reminding them of points on occasions and praising them when they get into the correct positions. With regular practice they will begin to do so quite easily.

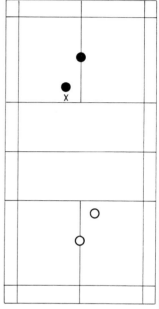

Figure 7.14

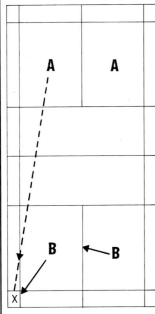

Figure 7.15

Positional rally practices

These are cooperative practices which begin with both teams positioned in the sides attacking formation in their MCs. They are easy to perform, but read through them carefully to make sure you teach them properly.

First Practice

Aim: To give the players experience of moving from a MC sides formation to a RC front and back attacking formation.

1. Name the teams A and B.
2. The teams rally in the MC. The shuttle should be hit horizontally and pass close to the net.
3. After several hits, one player from Team A lobs the shuttle to Team B's RC.
4. Team B position themselves to attack, and Team A position themselves to defend. See figure 7.15.
5. The Team B back player must smash (medium pace smash). The Team A defender must lob high to the RC or push or drive the shuttle horizontally across the net to the sides of the MC. The Team B back player must smash each time Team A lobs.
6. If Team A hit the shuttle to the sides of the MC, either the front or back player of Team B hits the shuttle back to Team A's MC and the players again take up the sides attacking formation.
7. The teams continue to rally for several hits until Team A again lobs the shuttle to the RC.

Comment: After five to ten minutes change the teams over. Give sufficient time for the players to perform the practice satisfactorily.

Second Practice

Aim: To give the players experience of moving from a sides formation to a FC front and back attacking formation.

1. The teams rally in the MC as in the previous practice.
2. After several hits one player from Team A hits the shuttle softly over the net into the FC and travels forward to act as the front player. See figure 7.16.
3. One player from Team B travels forward to hit the shuttle back as the front player.

Note: Both front players must let the shuttle fall below net height before they hit it and must return behind the short service line after hitting the shuttle.

4. The two front players rally for several hits until the player from Team A hits the shuttle (from above the net if necessary) towards the side of the MC and then travels back to take up a sides formation.

5. The back player of Team B hits the shuttle back to the MC of Team A as Team B's front player travels back into a sides formation. See figure 7.17

6. The teams continue to rally from the MC until Team A again hits the shuttle softly into the FC.

Comment: Allow five to ten minutes for the players to perform the practice satisfactorily.

Figure 7.16   **Figure 7.17**

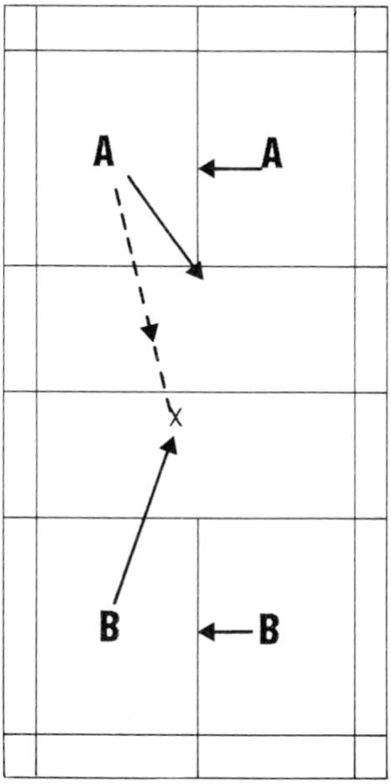

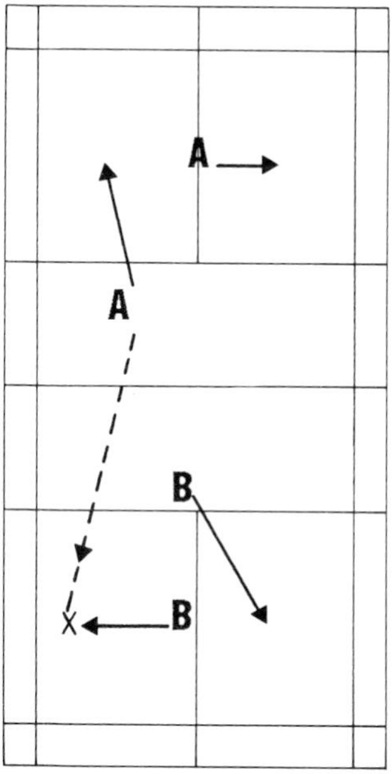

Play a Normal Game
Aim: To give the players experience of trying out their positional play in the game.
Comment: This time the teams can use the smash as a move. However, I would advise them to smash straight or to the centre. If they smash across court it is difficult for their front player to intercept the shuttle if the other team hit it straight down the line to the MC. See figure 7.18.

Skill Practices for Doubles

These are a mixture of cooperative and competitive practices which the players should find interesting and enjoyable.

Practice 1
The low serve and return of serve
Aim: To improve the performance of the low serve and return of serve
Instructions:
1. Players practise in pairs with A and B, C and D in the positions as shown in figure 7.19. The instructions for A and B also apply to C and D.
Note: the serve can be practised from the left or right side of the court
2. Player A serves low at or to the sides of Player B.
3. Player B practises the following replies away from the server (see figure 7.20.):
• Hit down the sides of FC
• Hit down the sides or centre of the MC
• Lob to the RC
4. The players take it in turn to practise the low serve and the replies.

Practice 2
The flick serve and return of serve
A flick serve is a fast serve used to catch out the receiver. The server prepares as if to serve low and then, just prior to hitting the

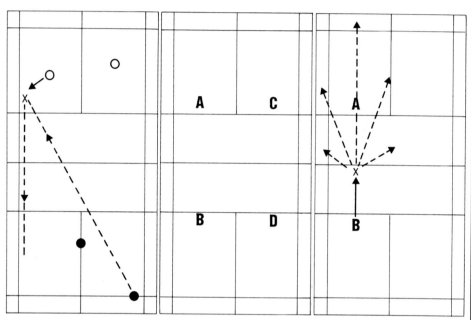

Figure 7.18   **Figure 7.19**   **Figure 7.20**

shuttle, accelerates the racket head to hit the shuttle quickly
above the receiver's reach to the RC.

Aim: To improve the performance of the replies and the flick
serve.

Instructions:

1. The players stand as in the previous practice
2. Player A prepares as if to serve a low serve and then hits the
shuttle quickly over Player B's head to catch Player B unprepared.
3. Player B tries to be alert and ready to smash the shuttle down
to the MC or clear it to the RC.
4. The players take it in turn to practise the flick serve and the
replies.

Practice 3

The low serve and flick serve

Aim: To develop players' skill in outwitting each other.

Instructions:

The players position themselves as before

1. Player A serves a low or flick serve to Player B.

2. Player B tries to keep alert in order to hit the shuttle down each time.

Note: If Player B has to lob or clear the shuttle then Player A has won the 'contest'.

Practice 4

MC sides attack practice

Aim: To improve skill in hitting the shuttle quickly across the net to the MC

Instructions:

1. The players work with a partner and stand opposite each other in their MCs.

2. They rally as fast as they can to hit the shuttle quickly horizontally across the net.

Note: For this practice they should adopt an alert attacking stance with the racket ready as a 'weapon' to hit the shuttle. See drawing opposite of the players ready to attack.

Comment: Let the players practise this until they feel competent at doing so.

Players ready to attack

Practice 5

Attack and defence

Aim: To improve the players' performance in the front and back attacking positions and in defense

Note: The attacking side must try to hit the shuttle to the ground while the defender tries to prevent them from doing so.

Instructions:

1. The players practise in threes in the half court. See figure 7.21
2. The defender serves high to the RC.
3. The back player smashes to the MC or drops to the FC.
4. The defender
    • In reply to the dropshot, lobs from FC
    • In reply to the smash, lobs to the RC or blocks to the FC or pushes or drives the shuttle to the MC
5. The attacking side must try to hit the shuttle to the ground; the defender must try to prevent them.

Comment: There are many similar sorts of practice which you can make up for yourself. Think carefully what your players need to improve in the game and then make up a practice on the sorts of things they will experience in the game.

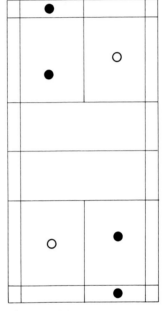

Figure 7.21

MIXED DOUBLES

Mixed Doubles

Mixed doubles is a subtle game in which both sides try to maintain the FC front and back attacking formation as much as possible. In this game the lady usually takes on the front-player role and the man the back-player role in order to make the most effective use of their relative strengths in the team. In fact, one of the main strategies in mixed doubles is to weaken the other team by trying to get the lady to the back and the man to the front. It will become apparent to you that this strategy provides the explanation for many of the positions adopted by the players and many of the tactics used in mixed doubles.

I will begin by giving a brief but sufficient description of how to play mixed doubles, illustrated with diagrams, before explaining how to teach it.

Forecourt Front and Back Attacking Formation

First look at figure 8.1 which shows the teams already in the FC front and back attacking formation with the lady about to serve to the lady.

Now imagine that the serving lady serves a low serve and the receiving lady steps forward and pushes the shuttle down to the MC, past the serving lady and just in front of her partner. See figure 8.2. The man on the serving side does not want to hit the

Figure 8.1   **Figure 8.2**

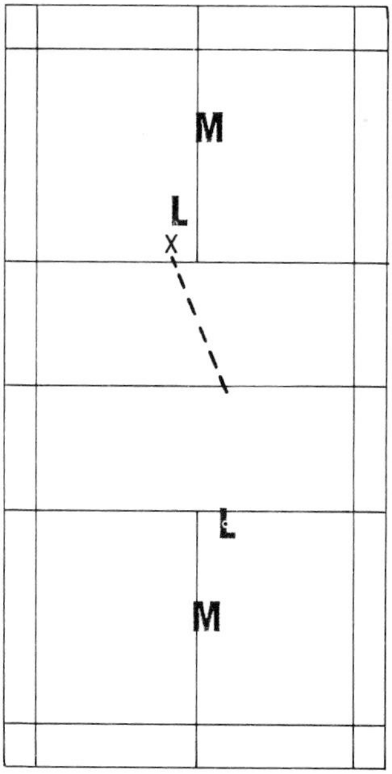

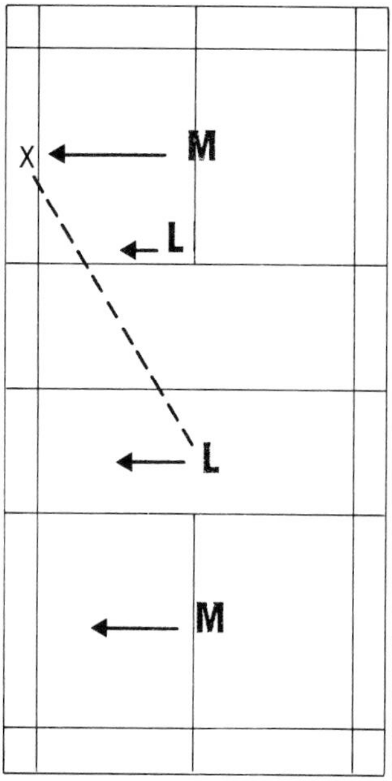

shuttle up and give the other team the chance to smash so he also tries to hit the shuttle down the line to the MC, past the opposing front lady and just in front of her man.

Both teams try to hit the shuttle low down the side of the court. I have illustrated this with the shaded area on figure 8.3. The obvious question you will now ask is: *If this is the case, then why doesn't the lady or the man simply step across to the side, intercept the shuttle and hit it down to the ground for a winner or to force the other side to lob it higher for an easy smash?*

Look again at figures 8.2 and 8.3 and let's imagine that the lady and the man tried to do this to you. They might get away with it the first time they did it but perhaps not the second time. I am sure that you would hit the shuttle across the court to the empty side if you thought for a moment that they were about to step towards

Figure 8.3   **Figure 8.4**   **Figure 8.5**

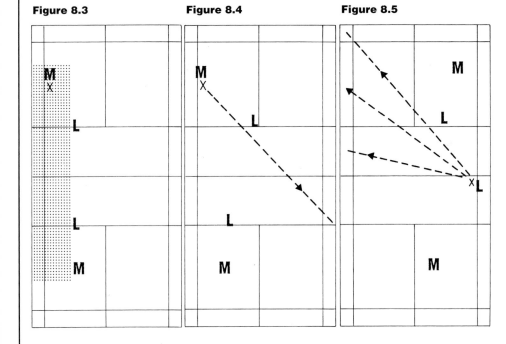

the line to intercept the shuttle. This is what a good mixed doubles' player would also do as figure 8.4 shows.

If you watch a good mixed doubles' contest you will see much 'cat and mouse' play down the side of the court along the shaded area with both teams:

• Trying to draw the other team out of position to one side of the court so that they can catch the other team out by hitting the shuttle to the empty space on the other side of the court.

• Trying to force the other team to hit the shuttle from near the ground and so hit it upwards for an easy smash.

• Trying to intercept without being caught out of position.

You can imagine that each team must possess patience, good control of the shuttle and skill in judging just the right moment to intercept the reply. This is particularly so for the front ladies of each team as they must continually threaten to intercept any replies, as well as cover a possible court move. The back man of each team has to hit the shuttle accurately down the line and skim the net to prevent the opposing front lady from hitting down. If she does intercept, he must also be ready to hit the shuttle quickly across the court if either of the other team tries to intercept too early.

Figure 8.5 illustrates where the shuttle is aimed across the court, i.e. to the RC, MC or FC, ideally played with a downward hit if possible.

Comment

This attacking formation, played from one side or other of the court, is the general pattern of play. There are occasions, however, when the situation may change, and one team will adopt a RC front and back attacking formation and the other team a sides defensive formation, as, for example, when the shuttle is lobbed or cleared to the RC. Though I have discussed this situation in level doubles (see Chapter 7) it becomes slightly more complex when it occurs in mixed doubles. The reason for this is, as I mentioned earlier, that each team tries to keep the lady as the front player and the man as the back player, and that to alter these positions weakens the strength of the team.

Rearcourt Front and Back Attacking Formation

The lady as the back player

This attack varies slightly depending on whether the lady or the man is the back player in this situation. If the lady is the back player then their team roles have been reversed and her task is to get into position as the front player as soon as she can. Let us look at how she might have been manoeuvred to the RC and what she does to take up the front-player role again.

Look at figure 8.6. The lady serves high to the lady and forces her out of position to the RC. The arrows show where the players travel to after the serve.

What stroke-moves can the lady play in this situation to regain her position as the front player? Look at the positions in the shaded area in figure 8.7 and you will see that she has three choices.

Figure 8.6

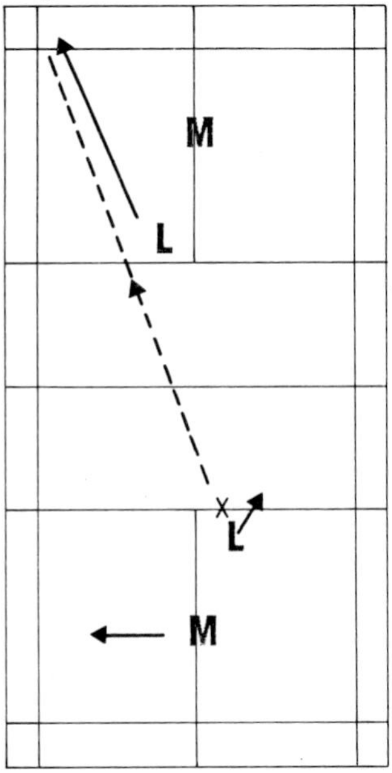

Figure 8.7

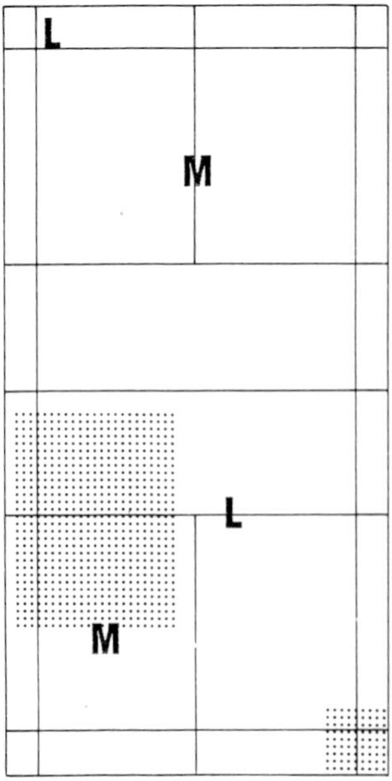

1. If she is strong enough, she can clear the shuttle cross court to the RC to move the opposing man as far away from the net as possible and to give her time to run forwards to the FC to defend against a possible cross-court smash from the man. figure 8.8 illustrates this.

2. She can hit the shuttle down to play a straight dropshot to the FC, or:

3. A straight smash to the MC and then run forwards to regain her position, and to cover the possible replies from the lady or the man. Figure 8.9 illustrates this. She will usually expect the lady to reply to her dropshot and the man to reply to her smash. If she is successful, then we should see both teams once again in the FC front and back attacking formation.

The man as the back player
There are two occasions when one team might place the other team in a RC front and back attacking formation with the man as the back player. First, when either the lady or the man serves to the opposing man; and second when the shuttle is hit cross-court

Figure 8.8   **Figure 8.9**

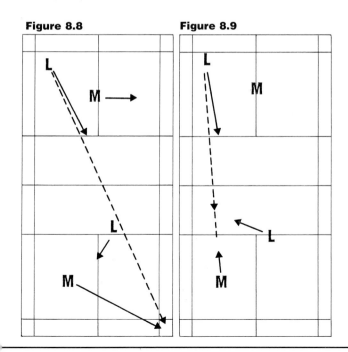

to the RC away from the opposing man, the 'cat and mouse' situation, or when the lady plays a cross court reply to the high serve. However it comes about, the situation is shown in figure 8.10.

I would like you to notice that in this situation the defending lady is positioned to cover the cross-court smash which is the general rule in mixed doubles.

To understand why, refer to figure 8.11 where I have positioned her to defend against the possible straight smash. Now remember what I said earlier about trying to reverse the positions of the man and the lady and consider how easy it is in this situation. All the man (or even the lady when she is the back player) has to do is clear the shuttle over the defending lady's head and she will be forced to travel out of position to the RC to make the reply. See figure 8.12 to see the results of the man's clear.

Now look at figure 8.13 with the lady positioned to defend against the cross-court smash. In this situation, should the man clear the shuttle to the lady's RC, she can simply leave it for her man to travel to. He is already positioned nearer the RC and can

Figure 8.10   **Figure 8.11**

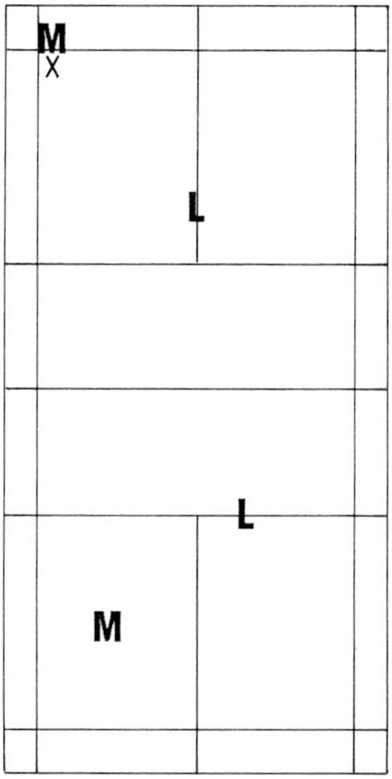

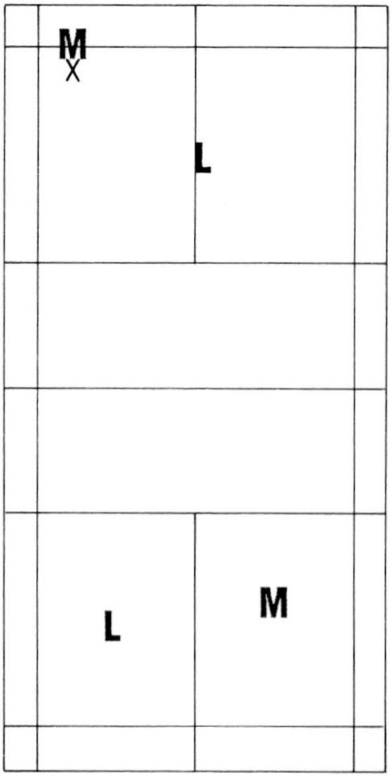

easily travel across the court to get into position for the reply.

I would like you also to notice that the opposing front lady now moves across the court to position herself for a possible cross court smash, while her partner also moves across the court to position himself for the straight smash.

Comments

At this point, if you are beginning to grasp some of the tactics and positional play of mixed doubles, you might want to pose several further questions.

Question One: Why does the defending lady position herself so far forward to defend against the smash?

Answer:

1. The position of the lady rules out the cross-court dropshot as a possible move and allows her partner to reply to the clear. In this position, therefore, she has only one move to reply to - the smash. The difficulty is that the shuttle travels very quickly and she must be alert and skilful to intercept it. However, her position is such

Figure 8.12   **Figure 8.13**

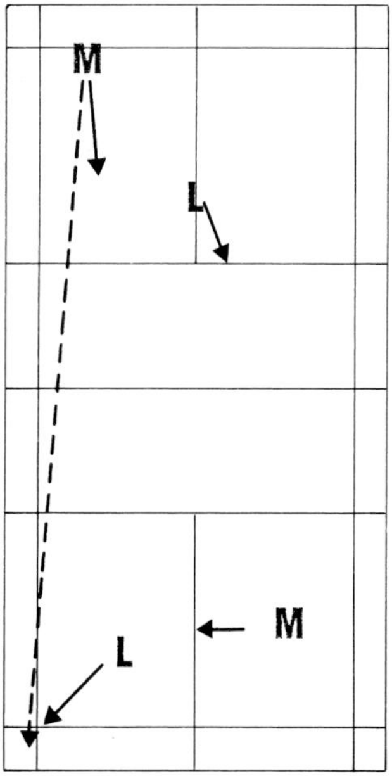

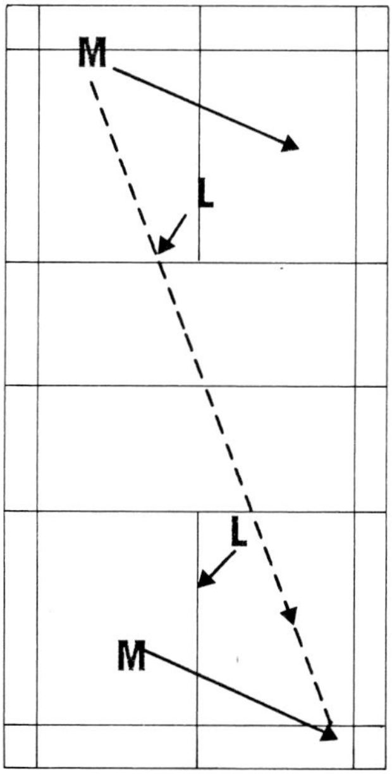

that the shuttle will be within her reach and, if she keeps her racket up, she can hit the shuttle down to the FC or MC for a possible winner. See figure 8.14.

2. Sometimes the lady does defend in the MC (see figure 8.15), usually when the opposing man's smash is so powerful that she finds it too difficult to stand so close to the net. By doing so she exposes herself to the dropshot, the fast clear over her head which she may now have to reply to, and the reply to the smash with the opposing front lady ready to intercept and hit down. It could be a weaker position relative to her own skill and that of the other team.

Comment: I would recommend that you teach your ladies to stand closer to the net near the FC.

Question Two: Where does the serving man's lady stand?
Answer: Look at figures 8.16 and 8.17 and you will see that she stands in front of him (as the front player) on his non-racket side, whether he serves to the right or the left court. He serves from the MC in order to maintain his position as the back player.

Figure 8.14   **Figure 8.15**   **Figure 8.16**

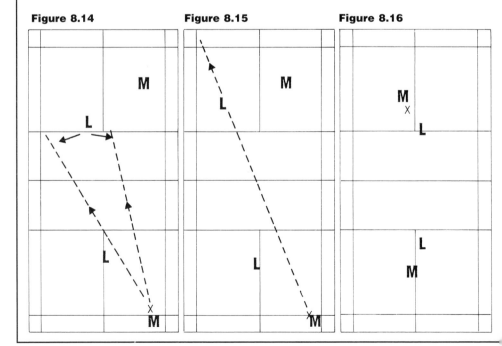

Question Three: Where does the receiving man's lady stand?
Answer: She can take up two positions:
1. First look at figure 8.18. In this instance she stands in front of him in order to retain her position as the front player. If the man now receives a low serve he must make a reply which allows him time to withdraw to the MC as the back player behind his lady. Hence he will try to hit the shuttle down into the FC or the MC so that the other team have to travel to it and hit it upwards. If he makes a move that the opponents can reply to by hitting the shuttle past him, there will be no one in position to cover it.
2. Now look at Figure 19. In this instance the lady is in the MC positioned behind the man. She adopts this position to allow her man to threaten and attack any low serve. She is now in position to cover any replies that get past her man.
Comment: I would recommend that you teach your beginners to play with the lady positioned in front of the man. It takes a very skilful and experienced lady to occupy the MC behind the man in their reversed positions.

Figure 8.17   **Figure 8.18**   **Figure 8.19**

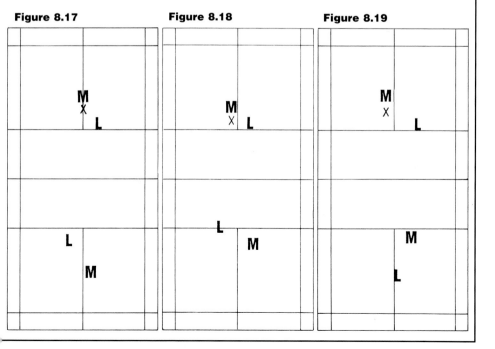

Coaching Mixed Doubles

First I would recommend that you read the above account of mixed doubles, give it some careful thought and then if possible go and watch some experienced players playing the game. See if they play the game as described here.

Second, I would recommend that you give your players a brief account of mixed doubles stressing the importance of the roles of the lady and the man and how they should combine as a team. Then let them have a game to experience mixed doubles while you observe them. As with level doubles, this will give you some points of reference for when you teach them to become better players.

Much of your coaching can take place while they play the game. You can stop them to make a point about their positions or the stroke-moves they use and with advice and encouragement they should make good progress. Their practice in singles and level doubles should contribute to their skill in mixed doubles. Even so there are several practices you can use to help them in certain parts of the game.

Practices for Mixed Doubles

First Practice

A very useful practice is one designed to improve their skill in the 'cat and mouse' situation described earlier. The players take up the FC front and back attacking formation. See figure 8.20.

1. The players rally down one side of the court with both teams trying to keep the shuttle low:
• To prevent the other team intercepting and hitting it down
• To force the other team to hit it up
• To draw the other team out of position and so create space for a winning cross-court move.

2. The other team will either intercept the cross-court move and hit the shuttle to the ground, in which case the rally starts again, or travel across the court to reach the shuttle and continue with the 'cat and mouse' rally down the other side.

Note: If at any time the rally is ended it begins again with the man in the MC serving down the line to the opposing man.

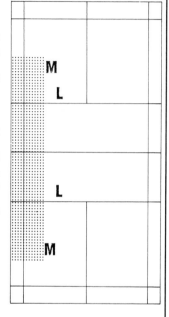

Figure 8.20

Second Practice

Aim: To improve the ladies' defence in the cross-court smash:

Instructions: The players position themselves as in figure 8.21. This is a cooperative practice.

1. The players practise in pairs: one man and one lady.
2. The lady serves high to the man in the RC and positions herself on the edge of the FC with her racket ready to hit the shuttle.
3. The man smashes straight at the lady who hits the shuttle straight down to the FC or MC.
4. The lady takes another shuttle and repeats the practice.
5. Allow the players to practise until the lady feels she is beginning to improve.
6. The ladies can now change over so that they receive cross-court smashes from the other side of the court.

General comments

Mixed doubles is a very popular game in clubs and sports centres and one which your players will want to learn and expect to play. The more you, as a coach, learn about it, the more you will be able to improve your players' skill and increase their understanding and enjoyment of the game. There is sufficient information here for you to do this.

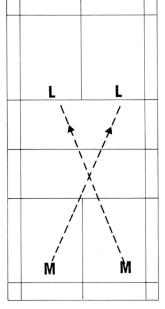

Figure 8.21

IMPROVING PERFORMANCE

Improving Performance

There are three main aspects of players' performance we are concerned with as coaches. These are: skill, fitness and attitude. In this book I have focused mainly on the players' skill and will continue to do so in this chapter. Even so you ought to know something about fitness and attitude as these are inter-related with skill. I will discuss each one briefly.

Fitness

All players have to be fit enough to do the work required to practise and play the game. Skill will be affected as players tire and players who are not fit enough to play risk damaging their health in some way, for example with injuries to muscles, tendons or ligaments or, in some cases, to their hearts. We have discussed the safety measures you ought to take to prevent the chance of injury occurring due to conditions in the hall you should also take some measures in advising players, particularly middle-aged adults, how to get fit enough to play badminton and avoid possible injury. These days there is sufficient information available on exercise, diet and fitness for you to read and advise your players. It is always wise to ask your players at the start if any have any injuries or illnesses which might be affected by playing. If there are any doubts about this ask the players concerned to seek medical advice before they play and/or to pace themselves carefully.

Basic Advice
• Advise your players to warm up before play, for example, ask them to put on a track suit and jog on the spot long enough to increase their heart rate slightly and warm their bodies. When they have done that they should do a few loosening, stretching exercises slowly, like arm circling, high knee raising, trunk twisting, and leg swinging backwards and forwards. They can conclude with a few shadow badminton movements, ie mime performing of the strokes.

In this way they can warm and stretch their muscles before

going on court to practise and play.

• After play advise them not to sit around in a damp shirt but to remove their shirt, dry off any surplus sweat and to put on a fresh shirt and a tracksuit or pullover.

• During practice and play, be alert for any player who appears to be getting out of breath too easily or is tiring too quickly. Advise them to pace themselves and take frequent rests until they get fitter through playing.

• Players who do get out of breath easily would benefit from regular exercise like jogging and walking to start with, gradually building up to 20 minutes continuous running or cycling about three times a week, providing they are not suffering from any heart illness, in which case their doctor's advice should be sought.

Attitude

I am concerned here with how the players behave in the game. Basically you want them to enjoy themselves, to get on well with the other players, to work hard in practice and to give a hundred percent effort in trying to win. In brief, to behave in ways which make the whole occasion a worthwhile and pleasurable one for all involved. Such players are fair, sporting and sociable.

What you don't want are players who behave in ways which lessen the enjoyment of the game, ie who get irritated, throw their rackets down, become bad tempered and rude, who cheat or continually question the honesty of other players, and do not try.

As a coach, part of your job is to develop acceptable attitudes in your players. This becomes more of a problem with younger players who may still be learning how to behave in sport and who place so much emphasis on winning that they adopt poor attitudes if they are not. They are also influenced by those sporting stars seen on TV whose poor behaviour they tend to copy as if it is alright to do so.

You can help to develop young players' attitudes by the example you set yourself. If you are considerate and show respect for your players, if you treat them fairly and are always honest with them and show you care about how they behave, then they are more likely to follow your example. You must use your experience and commonsense to judge whether or not your players' behaviour is acceptable, and if it is not, do not allow it. Tell the players but also explain why their behaviour is not acceptable. Above all be consistent and treat all the players equally in this respect.

You can also improve their concentration, determination and adventurousness in play by giving praise and encouragement when they do try hard, and by giving them practices to do which allow them to make progress and achieve something in the lesson. Everyone responds to their efforts being encouraged and their achievements (no matter how small) being acknowledged with praise - badminton players are no different.

Skill

When we talk about skill we usually infer that the players have reached a good standard of play - that they have become skilful. There are two areas in which we use the term:

• Technical skill - skill in using the racket and in moving on the court.

• Tactical skill - skill in using the strokes as moves to outwit the opponent.

You will recognize which of your players are technically skilful because they are more fluent, flowing, economical, effortless and stylish in their physical movements than other players. Similarly you will know which are tactically skilful as their use of strokes will be more intelligent and imaginative than others.

I have already provided many lessons on how to develop your players' tactical skill. In fact the main emphasis so far in this book has been on how to play the opponent - to make the three basic moves tactical moves. We have already covered many aspects of the players' technical skill: the basic grips, stroke cycle, the basic stances and starting position on the court and the basic stroke-moves. Your players have experienced performing many of the strokes already and should have reached a reasonable level of skill in doing so.

I think it will help you if we now consider a few of the more important features in performing some of the strokes and explain how to develop your players' skill in moving on the court.

Performing the Strokes

Previously I wrote that players should perform a stroke cycle for each stroke (see page xx). This comprises:

1. The racket starting position: This should be in front with the racket held in an alert grip and the hand cocked so lifting the racket head ready to hit the shuttle.

2. The preparation: From the starting position the racket head is taken back further ready to hit the shuttle. How much it is taken back depends on where the shuttle is and how hard the player wants to hit it.

When the shuttle is in front the player may only need to take the racket head back by cocking the hand.

If the shuttle is high and a strong hit is required, the player may take the racket head further by twisting the shoulders and lifting the racket arm back behind the shoulders into a throwing position which we call the **smash position**.

Below left: The racket starting position
Below right: The preparation

3. The hit: The racket head is now thrown forwards at the shuttle either upwards or sideways according to the shuttle position. For a strong hit players must accelerate the racket head forwards very quickly, whereas for a gentle hit a slower movement forwards will suffice. So from the preparation players simply hit the shuttle with more or less force in the direction they want it to go.

4. The recovery: On most forehand strokes the racket head will naturally continue forwards after the hit so the player hits through the shuttle. On the backhand side it is quite easy to check the racket head on impact with the shuttle and prevent any follow-through. This is particularly so on the high backhand. What is important is that players recover to the racket starting position after each hit in order to complete the stroke cycle.

Comment:
The throwing action used for many forehand strokes is one which players should master. It is the same action that is used when throwing a ball overarm, sidearm or underarm, except that the player throws the racket head at the shuttle. I will describe this action with the help of some illustrations.

The throwing action
This action is used primarily for overhead stroke-moves usually played from the rearcourt, ie the smash, clear and the dropshot. Ideally the player should get into position to be able to smash, **the smash position,** so forcing the opponents to take up a defensive stance and then perhaps catching the opponents out with a drop or clear instead. Below are a sequence of actions illustrating the throwing action performed in the smash.

Note that the player is turned sideways on to the shuttle when preparing to hit it and that the shuttle is struck from a high position in front of the player. See the sequence opposite.

The forehand smash:
1 Starting position, 2, 3, 4 and 5 Preparation, 6 , 7 and 8 Hit, 9 and 10 Follow-through and 11 Recovery.

106

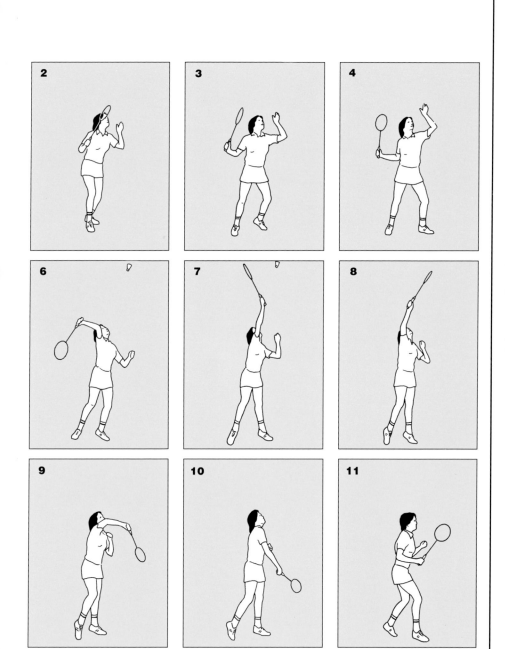

Overhead backhand clear
Top: Preparation
Above: Hit

The backhand clear

Most beginners find this difficult usually because they do not use the backhand grip and/or they try to hit the shuttle too hard and too far.

For this stroke the player prepares by twisting the shoulders to the backhand side to take the racket head back ready to hit the shuttle. The player is then positioned with his back to the net. The player then hits the shuttle by tapping it with the racket face. You should recognize the tap action because you will see a light quick action and the racket head rebound on impact with the shuttle.

After the hit the player immediately recovers the racket to the starting position.(See page xx.) The main point in teaching this stroke is to make sure that the players experience the rebound on impact with the shuttle. It doesn't matter at this stage whether or not the shuttle travels the full distance of the court. This can be achieved gradually as the player uses a stronger tap action.

The serve

As this is one of the opening moves in the game, players ought to practise regularly to improve. To some extent they will have done so every time they began a rally or served in a game. Nevertheless as it is an important stroke-move you should try to improve their performance of it.

The low serve

Look at the sequence opposite which shows the preparation, hit and follow through for the low serve. The player stands sideways about two to three feet from the front service line and holds the shuttle in front gently in the fingers.The racket head is swung gently forwards to **push** the shuttle forwards to skim the net and fall on to the front service line as the player's weight transfers onto the front foot. The racket recovers ready to threaten any reply.

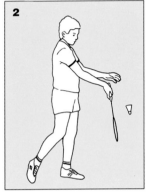

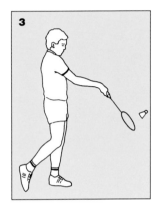

The low serve : 1
Preparation, 2 and 3 Hit, 4
Follow-through and 5
Recovery into the attack
position.

The high serve

The starting position is the same as for the low serve (see the low serve sequence of illustrations).

The hit: The player throws the racket downwards and forwards to hit upwards from below the falling shuttle, sending it high to the RC as the player's weight transfers onto the front foot.

The racket head follows through in the direction of the shuttle before recovering to its starting position ready for any replies.

Receiving the serve

Players should be ready to travel quickly forwards to attack the low serve and backwards to attack the high serve.

The stance is similar to the backward attacking stance described on page xx.

Players should adjust their position nearer to the front service line in doubles and further from it for singles.

The high serve: 1 Serving stance, 2 Hit, 3 Follow-through into recovery and 4 Recovery into defensive stance.

Moving on the Court

The players will have been moving around the court in practice and games and will have developed some skill in doing so. There are however some exercises you can use to improve their skill in moving. To do so you will need to develop a number of features: footwork, posture and balance, ability to start and stop quickly, and ability to change direction quickly. First I will give you some useful practices to improve general movement on the court.

Note: Most of the hitting in the MC and the FC is performed off the racket foot, the foot on the same side of the body as the hand which holds the racket. In the RC the racket foot is used to stop on and push off from onto the non-racket foot.

First practice
One step practice
See figure 9.1.

P (player) stands in the MC in the forward attacking stance.

F (the feeder) stands in the RC

Task: F must hit the shuttle within one step's reach of P - to the sides, in front and behind. P has to step onto his racket foot, hit the shuttle and return to the forward attacking stance.

The players rally until P feels competent at hitting off the racket foot. They change over.

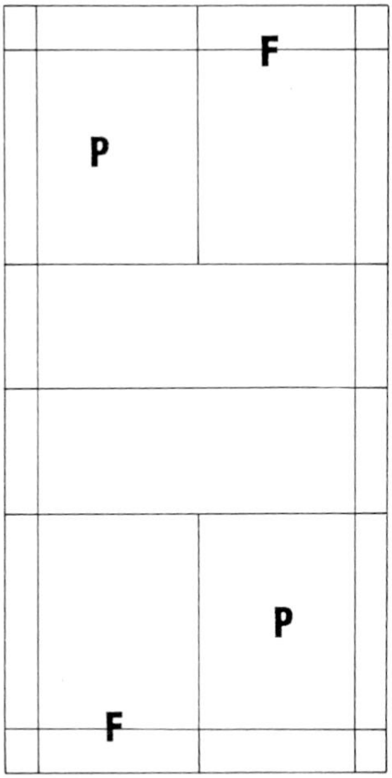

Figure 9.1

Second Practice
Travel and step practice
See figure 9.2 overleaf.

The players position themselves as before.

Task: F must hit the shuttle to the corners of the court or sides of the MC so that P must travel to hit the shuttle. When F hits the shuttle to the RC, P must travel and use the racket foot to stop on and hit off, or to push off from and transfer the body weight to hit the shuttle off the non-racket foot before recovering to the MC.

In the MC and FC, P will travel to arrive on and hit off the racket foot before recovering to the MC.

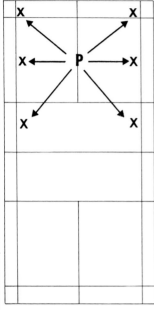

Figure 9.2

Third Practice

Shadow badminton practices

These practices are designed to improve certain features of movement.

Note: The players mime playing the game without a shuttlecock against an imaginary opponent. They play on the half court.

1. Quality of footwork

Task: Play at a comfortable pace without making a sound on the floor.

Comment: This exercise improves the lightness and quickness of movement.

2. Posture and balance

Task: Play keeping the trunk upright and the head up.

3. Starting and stopping

Task: Play showing a controlled stop in balance and a quick start to a new position.

Note: The player keeps moving, playing different strokes but pauses each time to show a controlled stop before performing each stroke and rapidly accelerating afterwards.

4. Changing direction

Task: Play, showing a smooth controlled change of direction when travelling in the court.

General comment:

Regular practise on these exercises will soon improve your players' skill in controlling their bodies and moving on the court.

LAWS OF BADMINTON

LAWS OF BADMINTON

LAWS OF BADMINTON

as revised in the year 1987 and adopted by THE INTERNATIONAL BADMINTON FEDERATION for introduction on 1st January 1988.

CONTENTS

1. COURT

1.1 The court shall be a rectangle and laid out as in the following Diagram 'A' (except in the case provided for in Law 1.5) and to the measurements there shown, defined by lines 40mm wide.

1.2 The lines shall be easily distinguishable and preferably be coloured white or yellow.

1.3.1 To show the zone in which a shuttle of correct pace lands when tested (Law 4.4), an additional four marks 40mm by 40mm may be made inside each line for singles of the right service court, 530mm and 990mm from the back boundary line.

1.3.2. In making these marks, their width shall be within the measurement given, i.e., the marks will be from 530mm to 570mm and from 950mm to 990mm from the outside of the back boundary line.

1.4 All lines form part of the area which they define.

1.5 Where space does not permit the marking out of a court for doubles, a court may be marked out for singles only as shown in Diagram 'B'. The back boundary lines become also the long service lines, and the posts, or the strips of material representing them (Law 2.2), shall be placed on the side lines.

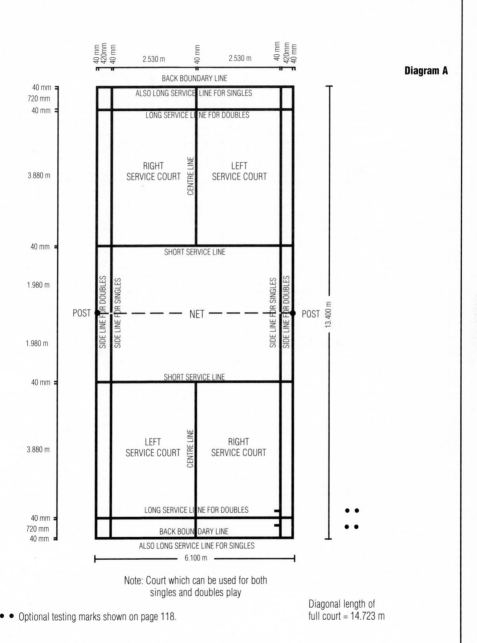

Diagram A

Note: Court which can be used for both
singles and doubles play

• • Optional testing marks shown on page 118.

Diagonal length of
full court = 14.723 m

115

**Optional Testing Marks for Doubles Court
(See Law 1.3)**

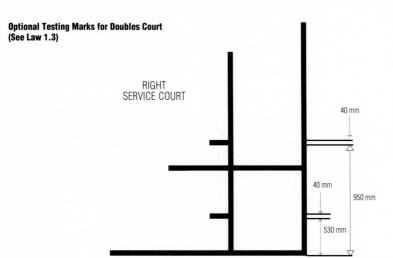

RIGHT
SERVICE COURT

40 mm

40 mm

950 mm

530 mm

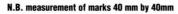

N.B. measurement of marks 40 mm by 40mm

**Optional Testing Marks for Singles Court
(See Law 1.3)**

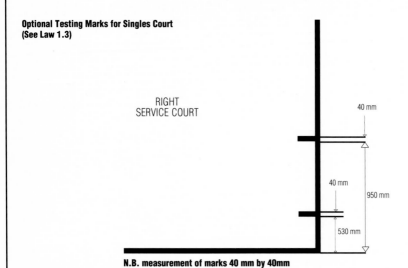

RIGHT
SERVICE COURT

40 mm

40 mm

950 mm

530 mm

N.B. measurement of marks 40 mm by 40mm

2. POSTS

2.1 The posts shall be 1.55 metres in height from the service of the court. They shall be sufficiently firm to remain vertical and to keep the net strained as provided in Law 3, and shall be placed on the doubles side lines as shown in Diagram 'A'.

2.2 Where it is not practicable to have posts on the side lines, some method must be used to indicate the position of the side lines where they pass under the net, e.g. by the use of the posts or strips of material 40mm wide, fixed to the side lines and rising vertically to the net cord.

2.3 On a court marked for doubles, the posts or strips of material representing the posts shall be placed on the side lines for doubles, irrespective of whether singles or doubles is being played.

3. NET

3.1 The net shall be made of fine cord of dark colour and even thickness with a mesh not less than 15mm and not more than 20mm.

3.2 The net shall be 760mm in depth.

3.3 The top of the net shall be edged with a 75mm white tape doubled over a cord or cable running through the tape. This tape must rest upon the cord or cable.

3.4 The cord or cable shall be of sufficient size and weight to be firmly stretched flush with the top of the posts.

3.5 The top of the net from the surface of the court shall be 1.524 metres at the centre of the court and 1.55 metres over the side lines for doubles.

3.6 There shall be no gaps between the ends of the nets and the posts. If necessary, the full depth of the net should be tied at the ends.

4. SHUTTLE

Principles
The shuttle may be made from natural and/or synthetic materials. Whatever material the shuttle is made from, the flight characteristics, generally, should be similar to those produced by a natural feathered shuttle with a cork base covered by a thin layer of leather.

Having regard to the Principles:
4.1 *General Design*
4.1.1 The shuttle shall have 16 feathers fixed in the base.

4.1.2 The feathers can have a variable length from 64mm to 70mm, but in each shuttle they shall be the same length when measured from the tip to the top of the base.

4.1.3 The tips of the feathers shall form a circle with a diameter from 58mm to 68mm.

4.1.4 The feathers shall be fastened firmly with thread or other suitable material.

4.1.5 The base shall be:
- 25mm to 28mm in diameter
- rounded on the bottom

4.2 *Weight*
The shuttle shall weight from 4.74 to 5.50 grams.

4.3 *Non-Feathered Shuttle*
4.3.1 The skirt or simulation of feathers in synthetic materials, replaces natural feathers.

4.3.2 The base is described in Law 4.1.5.

4.3.3 Measurements and weight shall be as in Law 4.1.2, 4.1.3 and 4.2. However, because of the difference of the specific gravity and behaviour of synthetic materials in comparison with feathers, a variation of up to ten per cent is acceptable.

4.4 *Shuttle Testing*
4.4.1 To test a shuttle, use a full underhand stroke which makes contact with the shuttle over the back boundary line. The shuttle shall be hit at an upward angle and in a direction parallel to the side lines.

4.4.2 A shuttle of correct pace will land not less than 530mm and not more than 990mm short of the other back boundary line.

4.5 *Modifications*
Subject to there being no variation in the general design, pace and flight of the shuttle, modifications in the above specifications may be made with the approval of the National Organization concerned:
4.5.1 in places where atmospheric conditions due to either altitude or climate make the standard shuttle unsuitable; or

4.5.2 if special circumstances exist which make it otherwise necessary in the interests of the game.

5. RACKET

5.1 The hitting surface of the racket shall be flat and consist of a pattern of crossed strings connected to the frame and either alternately interlaced or bonded where they cross. The stringing pattern shall be generally uniform and, in particular, not less dense in the centre than in any other area.

5.2 The frame of the racket, including the handle, shall not exceed 680mm in overall length and 230mm in overall width.

5.3 The overall length of the head shall not exceed 290mm.

5.4 The strung surface shall not exceed 280mm in overall length and 220mm in overall width.

5.5 *The racket:*
5.5.1 shall be free of attached objects and protrusions, other than those used solely and specifically to limit or prevent wear and tear, or vibration, or to distribute weight, or to secure the handle by cord to the player's hand, and which are reasonable in size and placement for such purposes; and

5.5.2 shall be free of any device which makes it possible for a player to change materially the shape of the racket.

6. APPROVED EQUIPMENT

The International Badminton Federation shall rule on any question of whether any racket, shuttle or equipment or any prototypes used in the playing of Badminton complies with the specifications or is otherwise approved or not approved for play. Such ruling may be undertaken on the Federation's initiative or upon application by any party with a bona fide interest therein including any player, equipment manufacturer or National Organization or member thereof.

Diagram B

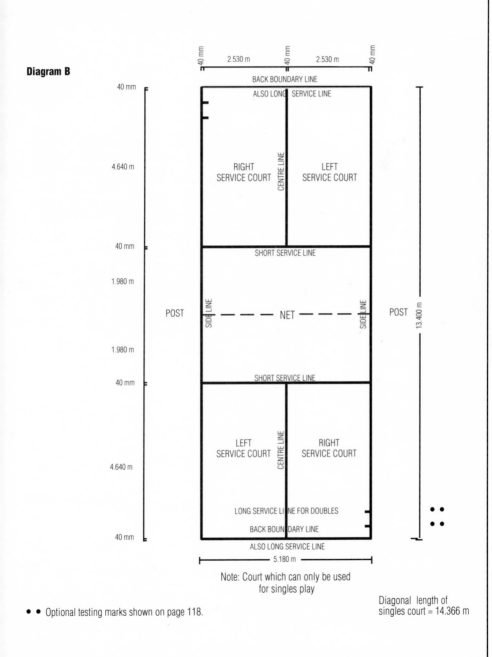

Note: Court which can only be used for singles play

• • Optional testing marks shown on page 118.

Diagonal length of singles court = 14.366 m

LAWS OF BADMINTON

7. PLAYERS

7.1 'Player' applies to all those taking part in a match.

7.2 The game shall be played, in the case of doubles, by two players a side, or in the case of singles, by one player a side.

7.3 The side having the right to serve shall be called the serving side, and the opposing side shall be called the receiving side.

8. TOSS

8.1 Before commencing play, the opposing sides shall toss and the side winning the toss shall exercise the choice in either Law 8.1.1 or Law 8.1.2.

    8.1.1 To serve or receive first.

    8.1.2 To start play at one end of the court or the other.

8.2 The side losing the toss shall then exercise the remaining choice.

9. SCORING

9.1 The opposing sides shall play the best of three games unless otherwise arranged.

9.2 Only the serving side can add a point to its score.

9.3 In doubles and Men's singles a game is won by the first side to score 15 points, except as provided in Law 9.6.

9.4 In Ladies' singles a game is won by the first side to score 11 points, except as provided in Law 9.6.

9.5
    9.5.1 If the score becomes 13 all or 14 all (9 all or 10 all in Ladies' singles), the side which first scored 13 or 14 (9 or 10) shall have the choice of 'setting' or 'not setting' the game (Law 9.6).

    9.5.2 This choice can only be made when the score is first reached and must be made before the next service is delivered

    9.5.3 The relevant side (Law 9.5.1) is given the opportunity to set at 14 all (10 all in Ladies' singles) despite any previous decision not to set by that side or the opposing side at 13 all (9 all in Ladies' singles).

9.6 If the game has been set, the score is called 'Love All' and the side first scoring the set number of points (Law 9.6.1 to 9.6.4) wins the game.

9.6.1 13 all setting to 5 points

9.6.2 14 all setting to 3 points

9.6.3 9 all setting to 3 points

9.6.4 10 all setting to 2 points

9.7 The side winning a game serves first in the next game.

10. CHANGE OF ENDS

10.1 Players shall change ends:
10.1.1 at the end of the first game

10.1.2 prior to the beginning of the third game (if any); and:

10.1.3 in the third game, or in a one game match, when the leading score reaches:
- 6 in a game of 11 points
- 8 in a game of 15 points

10.2 When players omit to change ends as indicated by Law 10.1, they shall do so immediately the mistake is discovered and the existing score shall stand.

11. SERVICE

11.1 In a correct service:
11.1.1 neither side shall cause undue delay to the delivery of service;

11.1.2 the server and receiver shall stand within diagonally opposite service courts without touching the boundary lines of these service courts; some part of both feet of the server and receiver must remain in contact with the surface of the court in a stationary position until the service is delivered (Law 11.4);

11.1.3 the server's racket shall initially hit the base of the shuttle while the whole of the shuttle is below the server's waist;

11.1.4 the shaft of the server's racket at the instant of hitting the shuttle shall be pointing in a downward direction to such an extent that the whole of the head of the racket is discernibly below the whole of the server's hand holding the racket;

11.1.5 the movement of the server's racket must continue forwards after the start of the service (Law 11.2) until the service is delivered; and

11.1.6 the flight of the shuttle shall be upwards from the server's racket to pass over the net, so that, if not intercepted, it falls in the receiver's service court.

11.2 Once the players have taken their positions, the first forward movement

LAWS OF BADMINTON

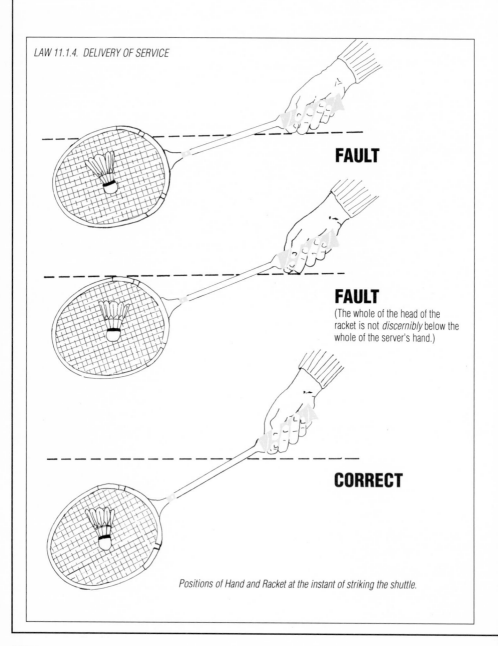

LAW 11.1.4. DELIVERY OF SERVICE

FAULT

FAULT
(The whole of the head of the racket is not *discernibly* below the whole of the server's hand.)

CORRECT

Positions of Hand and Racket at the instant of striking the shuttle.

of the server's racket is the start of the service.

11.3 The server shall not serve before the receiver is ready, but the receiver shall be considered to have been ready if a return of serve is attempted.

11.4 The service is delivered when, once started (Law 11.2), the shuttle is hit by the server's racket or the shuttle lands on the floor.

11.5 In doubles, the partners may take up any positions which do not unsight the opposing server or receiver.

12. SINGLES

12.1 The players shall serve from, and receive in, their respective right service courts when the server has not scored or has scored an even number of points in that game.

12.2 The players shall serve from, and receive in, their respective left service courts when the server has scored an odd number of points in that game.

12.3 If a game is set, the total points scored by the server in that game shall be used to apply Laws 12.1 and 12.2.

12.4 The shuttle is hit alternately by the server and the receiver until a 'fault' is made or the shuttle ceases to be in play.

12.5
12.5.1 If the receiver makes a 'fault' or the shuttle ceases to be in play because it touches the surface of the court inside the receiver's court, the server scores a point. The server then serves again from the alternate service court.

12.5.2 If the server makes a 'fault' or the shuttle ceases to be in play because it touches the surface of the court inside the server's court, the server loses the right to continue serving, and the receiver then becomes the server, with no point served by either player.

13. DOUBLES

13.1 At the start of the game, and each time a side gains the right to serve, the service shall be delivered from the right service court.

13.2 Only the receiver shall return the service: should the shuttle touch or be hit by the receiver's partner, the serving side scores a point.

13.3
13.3.1 After the service is returned, the shuttle is hit by either player of the serving side and then by either player of the receiving side, and so on, until the shuttle ceases to be in play.

13.3.2 After the service is returned, a player may hit the shuttle from any position on that player's side of the net.

13.4
13.4.1 If the receiving side makes a 'fault' or the shuttle cease to be in play because it touches the surface of the court inside the receiving side's court, the serving side scores a point, and the server serves again.

13.4.2 If the serving side makes a 'fault' or the shuttle ceases to be in play because it touches the surface of the court inside the serving side's court, the server loses the right to continue serving with no point scored by either side.

13.5

13.5.1 The player who serves at the start of any game shall serve from, or receive in, the right service court when that player's side has not scored or has scored an even number of points in that game, and the left service court otherwise.

13.5.2 The player who receives at the start of any game shall receive in, or serve from, the right service court when that player's side has not scored or has scored an even number of points in that game, and the left service court otherwise.

13.5.3 The reverse pattern applies to the partners.

13.5.4 If a game is set, the total points scored by a side in that game shall be used to apply Laws 13.5.1 to 13.5.3.

13.6 Service in any turn of serving shall be delivered from alternate service courts, except as provided in Laws 14 and 16.

13.7 The right to serve passes consecutively from the initial server in any game to the initial receiver in that game, and then consecutively from that player to that player's partner and then to one of the opponents and then the opponent's partner, and so on.

13.8 No player shall serve out of turn, receive out of turn, or receive two consecutive services in the same game, except as provided in Laws 14 and 16.

13.9 Either player of the winning side may serve first in the next game and either player of the losing side may receive.

14. SERVICE COURT ERRORS

14.1 A service court error has been made when a player:

14.1.1 has served out of turn

14.1.2 has served from the wrong service court: or

14.1.3 standing in the wrong service court, was prepared to receive the service and it has been delivered.

14.2 When a service court error has been made, then:

14.2.1 if the error is discovered before the next service is delivered, it is a 'let' unless only one side was at fault and lost the rally, in which case the error shall not be corrected.

14.2.2 if the error is not discovered before the next service is delivered, the error shall not be corrected.

14.3 If there is a 'let' because of a service court error, the rally is replayed with the error corrected.

14.4 If a service court error is not corrected, play in that game shall proceed without changing the players' new service courts (nor, when relevant, the new order of serving).

15. FAULTS

It is a 'fault':
15.1 if a service is not correct (Law 11.1)

15.2 if the server, in attempting to serve, misses the shuttle;

15.3 if after passing over the net on service, the shuttle is caught in or on the net;

15.4 if in play, the shuttle:
15.4.1 lands outside the boundaries of the court;

15.4.2 passes through or under the net;

15.4.3 fails to pass the net;

15.4.4 touches the roof, ceiling, or side walls;

15.4.5 Touches the person or dress of a player; or

15.4.6 touches any object or person outside the immediate surroundings of the court:
(Where necessary on account of the structure of the building, the local badminton authority may, subject to the right of veto of its National Organization, make bye-laws dealing with cases in which a shuttle touches an obstruction).

15.5 if, when in play, the initial point of contact with the shuttle is not on the striker's side of the net. (The striker may, however, follow the shuttle over the net with the racket in the course of a stroke.)

15.6 if, when the shuttle is in play, a player:

15.6.1 touches the net or its supports with racket, person or dress;

15.6.2 invades an opponent's court with racket or person in any degree except as permitted in Law 15.5; or

15.6.3 prevents an opponent from making a legal stroke where the shuttle is followed over the net;

15.7 if, in play, a player deliberately distracts an opponent by any action such as shouting or making gestures;

15.8 if, in play, the shuttle:

15.8.1 be caught and held on the racket and then slung during the execution of a stroke;

15.8.2 be hit twice in succession by the same player with two strokes; or

15.8.3 be hit by a player and the player's partner successively; or

15.9 if a player is guilty of flagrant, repeated or persistent offences under Law 18.

16. LETS

'Let' is called by the Umpire, or by a player (if there is no Umpire) to halt play.

16.1 A 'let' may be given for any unforeseen or accidental occurrence.

16.2 If a shuttle, after passing over the net, is caught in or on the net, it is a 'let' except during service.

16.3 If during service, the receiver and server are both faulted at the same time, it shall be a 'let'.

16.4 If the server serves before the receiver is ready it shall be a 'let'.

16.5 If during play, the shuttle disintegrates and the base completely separates from the rest of the shuttle, it shall be a 'let'.

16.6 If a Line Judge is unsighted and the Umpire is unable to make a decision, it shall be a 'let'.

16.7 When a 'let' occurs, the play since the last service shall not count, and the player who served shall serve again, except when Law 14 is applicable.

LAWS OF BADMINTON

17. SHUTTLE NOT IN PLAY

A shuttle is not in play when:

17.1 it strikes the net and remains attached there or suspended on top;

17.2 it strikes the net or post and starts to fall towards the surface of the court on the striker's side of the net;

17.3 it hits the surface of the cour; or

17.4 a 'fault' or 'let' has occurred.

18. CONTINUOUS PLAY, MISCONDUCT, PENALTIES

18.1 Play shall be continuous from the first service until the match is concluded, except as allowed in Laws 18.2 and 18.3.

18.2 An interval not exceeding 5 minutes is allowed between the second and third games of all matches in all the following situations:

18.2.1 in international competitive events;

18.2.2 in IBF sanctioned events; and

18.2.3 in all other matches (unless the National Organization has previously published a decision not to allow such an interval).

18.3 When necessitated by circumstances not within the control of the players, the Umpire may suspend play for such a period as the Umpire may consider necessary. If play be suspended, the existing score shall stand and play be resumed from that point.

18.4 Under no circumstances shall play be suspended to enable a player to recover his strength or wind, or to receive instruction or advice.

18.5
18.5.1 Except in the intervals provided in Laws 18.2 and 18.3, no player shall be permitted to receive advice during a match.

18.5.2 Except at the conclusion of a match, no player shall leave the court without the Umpire's consent.

18.6 The Umpire shall be the sole judge of any suspension of play.

18.7 A player shall not:

18.7.1 deliberately cause suspension of play;

18.7.2 deliberately interfere with the speed of the shuttle;

18.7.3 behave in an offensive manner; or

18.7.4 be guilty of misconduct not otherwise covered by the Laws of Badminton.

18.8 The Umpire shall administer any breach of Law 18.4, 18.5 or 18.7 by:

18.8.1 issuing a warning to the offending side;

18.8.2 faulting the offending side, if previously warned; or

18.8.3 in cases of flagrant offence or persistent offences, faulting the offending side and reporting the offending side immediately to the Referee, who shall have the power to disqualify.

18.9 Where a Referee has not been appointed, the responsible official shall have the power to disqualify.

19. OFFICIALS AND APPEALS

19.1 The Referee is in overall charge of the tournament or event of which a match forms part.

19.2 The Umpire, where appointed, is in charge of the match, the court and its immediate surrounds. The Umpire shall report to the Referee. In the absence of a Referee, the Umpire shall report instead to the responsible official.

19.3 The Service Judge shall call service faults made by the server should they occur (Law 11).

19.4 A Line Judge shall indicate whether a shuttle is 'in' or 'out'.

An Umpire shall:
19.5 uphold and enforce the Laws of Badminton and, especially call a 'fault' or 'let' should either occur, without appeal being made by the players;

19.6 give a decision on any appeal regarding a point of dispute, if made before the next service is delivered;

19.7 ensure players and spectators are kept informed of the progress of the match;

19.8 appoint or remove Line Judges or a Service Judge in consultation with the Referee;

19.9 not overrule the decisions of the Line Judges and the Service Judge on points of fact;

19.10
  19.10.1 where another court official is not appointed, arrange for their duties to be carried out;

  19.10.2 where an appointed official is unsighted, carry out the official's duties or play a 'let';

19.11 decide upon any suspension of play;

19.12 record and report to the Referee all matters in relation to Law 18; and

19.13 take to the Referee all unsatisfied appeals on questions of Law only.
(Such appeals must be made before the next service is delivered, or, if at the end of a game, before the side that appeals has left the court.)

LAWS OF BADMINTON

THIS BOOK HAS SHOWN THE IMPORTANT AND WIDE-RANGING ROLE OF THE COACH. IT HAS ALSO INDICATED THE KNOWLEDGE REQUIRED TO BE AN EFFECTIVE AND SUCCESSFUL COACH. THE SCOPE OF THIS BOOK CANNOT COVER EVERY TOPIC IN DETAIL, SO IF YOU HAVE DEVELOPED AN INTEREST IN SOME ASPECT OF COACHING SUCH AS MENTAL PREPARATION, FITNESS TRAINING OR THE PREVENTION OF INJURY, THE **NATIONAL COACHING FOUNDATION**, ESTABLISHED TO PROVIDE A SERVICE FOR SPORTS COACHES, RUNS COURSES, PRODUCES STUDY PACKS, BOOKS, VIDEOS AND OTHER RESOURCES ON MANY PERFORMANCE RELATED AREAS PARTICULARLY DESIGNED FOR THE PRACTISING COACH.

CONTACT THE **NATIONAL COACHING FOUNDATION** AT: 4 COLLEGE CLOSE, BECKETT PARK, LEEDS LS6 3QH. TELEPHONE: LEEDS (0532) 744802

CONTACT THE BADMINTON ASSOCIATION OF ENGLAND FOR INFORMATION ON HOW TO BECOME A QUALIFIED COACH AT:
BRADWELL ROAD, LOUGHTON LODGE, MILTON KEYNES.
TELEPHONE: (0908) 568822